LOW
GI
DIET
COOKBOOK

THE LOW GI DIET COOKBOOK

More than 70 delicious and
nutritious low-GI recipes
shown in over 300 photographs

Edited by Maggie Pannell

LORENZ BOOKS

NOTES

Bracketed terms are intended for American readers.

For all recipes, quantities are given in both metric and imperial measures and, where appropriate, in standard cups and spoons. Follow one set of measures, but not a mixture, because they are not interchangeable.

Standard spoon and cup measures are level. 1 tsp = 5ml, 1 tbsp = 15ml, 1 cup = 250ml/8fl oz.

Australian standard tablespoons are 20ml. Australian readers should use 3 tsp in place of 1 tbsp for measuring small quantities.

American pints are 16fl oz/2 cups. American readers should use 20fl oz/ 2.5 cups in place of 1 pint when measuring liquids.

Electric oven temperatures in this book are for conventional ovens. When using a fan oven, the temperature will probably need to be reduced by about 10–20°C/20–40°F. Since ovens vary, you should check with your manufacturer's instruction book for guidance.

The nutritional analysis given for each recipe is calculated per portion (i.e. serving or item), unless otherwise stated. If the recipe gives a range, such as Serves 4–6, then the nutritional analysis will be for the smaller portion size, i.e. 6 servings. The analysis does not include optional ingredients, such as salt added to taste.

Medium (US large) eggs are used unless otherwise stated.

Main front cover image shows Grilled Halloumi and Bean Salad – for recipe, see page 44

This edition is published by Lorenz Books, an imprint of Anness Publishing Ltd,
Blaby Road, Wigston,
Leicestershire LE18 4SE; info@anness.com

www.lorenzbooks.com; www.annesspublishing.com

If you like the images in this book and would like to investigate using them for publishing, promotions or advertising, please visit our website www.practicalpictures.com for more information.

Publisher: Joanna Lorenz
Project Editor: Lucy Doncaster
Copy Editor: Maggie Pannell
Designer: Nigel Partridge
Production Controller: Wendy Lawson

© Anness Publishing Ltd 2013

PUBLISHER'S NOTE
Although the advice and information in this book are believed to be accurate and true at the time of going to press, neither the authors nor the publisher can accept any legal responsibility or liability for any errors or omissions that may have been made nor for any inaccuracies nor for any loss, harm or injury that comes about from following instructions or advice in this book.

The diets and information in this book are not intended to replace advice from a qualified practitioner, doctor or dietician. Always consult your health practitioner before adopting any of the suggestions in this book. Neither the author nor the publisher can accept any liability for failure to follow this advice.

While every attempt has been made to accurately input the ingredients and their weights into a software package, there are not Glycemic Index values available for all of the ingredients listed. The Glycaemic load value per serving is shown as a guide only.

CONTENTS

What is the GL Diet?

Just when you thought you were getting to grips with GI (the Glycaemic Index), along comes yet another term – GL, which stands for Glycaemic Load. Are you confused? Well hopefully not for much longer, as this book is designed to explain simply and clearly the meaning of these terms, and how a diet based on a system that considers the effect of different carbohydrate foods on blood sugar levels is an effective and healthy method of losing weight that is now recognized and recommended by nutrition professionals.

The Glycaemic Index

This is a numerical system that grades different carbohydrate foods according to the speed at which they are digested and converted to sugar (glucose), thus affecting blood sugar levels and the amount of readily available energy. This index only relates to carbohydrate foods and it is therefore this food group that is the main focus of the diet, although you must also watch your fat intake and take regular exercise for successful and maintained weight loss.

Below: Starchy carbohydrates should be your main source of energy.

The Glycaemic Load

This is a development of the GI index. It is based on GI values, but a further calculation is made which takes into consideration the actual amount of carbohydrate eaten in a typical serving size of the food, or how many 'carbs' there are in an average portion, so it provides a more useful guide. It is also more accurate and more effective than following GI values, which can sometimes be misleading as they are calculated purely on the quality and not the quantity of carbohydrate present in an average-sized portion of the food.

How GI and GL values are calculated and the differences between them will be explained in greater detail later.

All about carbohydrates

Carbohydrates are just one of the five nutrient groups of which food is made up. The others are proteins, fats, vitamins and minerals. All these nutrients are found in different foods and serve various functions in the body. It is, therefore, important that we eat a wide variety of foods to help to keep us fit and healthy. Health and weight problems arise when nutrients are out of balance, whether in an insufficient or excess quantity.

Above: Choose whole fruit, rather than juice, for their fibre value.

Carbohydrates provide the most readily available form of energy for all the activities of the body, and they are present in varying amounts in different foods. They can be divided into three groups – sugars, starches and fibre – which are defined according to their individual chemical structure. Various sugars and starches take different times to be broken down and digested.

Sugars have a simple chemical structure and this group is further divided into monosaccharides (called simple sugars), including glucose and fructose (fruit sugar), found naturally in fruit and sweet-tasting vegetables; and disaccharides, including sucrose (table sugar) and lactose, which is a naturally occurring sugar found in milk.

Starches have a more complex molecular structure but it's now known that the speed at which they are broken down during digestion to release glucose depends on the structure of the starch. Starchy carbohydrate foods include grains, in the form of bread,

THE GL PRINCIPLE

Carbohydrate foods with a low GL take longer to digest, help keep blood sugar levels stable and provide a steady release of energy. They are therefore ideal foods on which to base a healthy diet, both for weight loss and a long-term maintenance plan.

pasta, oats, breakfast cereals and couscous etc., rice, pulses (peas, beans and lentils), potatoes and other starchy vegetables.

Fibre is not a digestible material, but simply provides bulk and promotes a healthy gut by assisting the passage of digestible materials and waste products through the intestines. There are two types of fibre present in plant foods – soluble and insoluble – and although both are essential for a healthy digestion, it is the soluble type, mainly present in oats, beans, peas, lentils and most fruit and vegetables, that has the added benefit of helping to control blood sugar levels by slowing down the absorption of glucose. Many foods with a low GI contain soluble fibre.

Other nutrients, namely fat and protein, as well as the fibre value present in the food, affect speed of digestion. This is also affected by the degree to which a food has been refined or processed.

All these foods have a differing effect on blood sugar levels and it is this glycaemic response on which the GI index and GL values are based.

Carbohydrates in the diet

Starchy carbohydrates, especially wholegrain varieties, are dietary staples and they should form the basis of a healthy diet. These foods also help to provide protein, vitamins, minerals and fibre and are very low in fat in their natural state.

You should choose wholegrain varieties as much as possible, because when carbohydrates are refined or processed, such as in white flour, bread, rice and pasta, much of the fibre and nutrient value is stripped away.

Severely restricting carbohydrates upsets the metabolic balance and can leave you feeling tired and unwell, causing complaints such as constipation, headaches and bad breath. Long term, a very low carbohydrate diet is difficult to stick to and does not retrain your eating habits, so the weight is likely to pile back on again afterwards.

Above: Different carbohydrate foods are digested at different speeds.

Carbohydrates not needed for immediate energy are converted into glycogen and stored in the liver and muscles for future energy use, or may be stored as body fat. However, if the body is continually supplied with too much readily available energy, not only is more fat accumulated but the body cannot draw on its existing stored energy sources.

Regulating blood sugar

Keeping blood sugar levels stable and providing a steady release of energy is the key to healthy eating and losing weight successfully. This means choosing 'good carbs' and is why the GL index provides the answer.

During digestion, carbohydrates are converted to glucose and the hormone insulin is released into the bloodstream to utilize this sugar as a source of energy. However, if blood sugar levels are high, as a result of regularly eating the type of carbohydrate foods that are readily converted to glucose, extra insulin is produced to 'mop up' this excess sugar, causing blood sugar levels to plummet. This results in tiredness and prompts the desire to snack. This causes a pattern of yo-yoing blood sugar, commonly called the sugar trap, to develop.

As snacks tend to be carbohydrate foods that are high in sugar and fat, like chocolate, biscuits (cookies) and crisps (US potato chips), it's easy to see how one can quickly consume excess calories and fail to lose weight.

The rationale of the GI and GL diet, therefore, is about keeping blood sugar levels on a more even keel, so hunger is controlled, you feel satisfied for longer and there's less temptation to snack between meals.

GL DIET BENEFITS

- It is a healthy method of dieting.
- It includes a wide variety of foods.
- Although certain foods should be eaten in moderation, no foods are banned.
- It is easy to follow and adapt to.
- Recipes are delicious.
- You will feel satisfied and not crave snacks between meals.
- It is family friendly.
- You can eat out and entertain with ease.
- Excess weight will drop off and stay off for good.
- It is helpful for improving many health conditions, as well as for losing weight.

How foods are categorized

We now know that carbohydrate foods take different times to be digested and consequently vary in their effect on blood sugar and insulin levels. This is measured by the GI index, so before discussing how GL values are calculated, it is necessary first to explain how the GI index of carbohydrates was devised.

The GI index

This index was developed following scientific experiments on healthy people. The volunteers were fed different carbohydrate foods, then the digestion time for each food to be converted into glucose was measured by taking blood sugar readings at regular intervals. Glucose was usually used as the control, as this is the simple molecule into which all other carbohydrates are broken down and is therefore the most readily absorbed. Glucose was given a value of 100, to be used as the standard against which all other carbohydrate foods were measured on a ranking scale of 0 to 100.

The actual quantity of each food eaten varied enormously as it had to provide 50g/2oz of useable carbohydrate. For a vegetable like carrots, this meant eating a large amount, as they do not contain much carbohydrate. For a carbohydrate food that is high in starch, such as pasta, a smaller portion size provided the 50g/2oz required. Foods were designated a number according to their average glycaemic response and hence the GI index was drawn up.

However, there is no definitive GI table. Values vary slightly depending on the source of the information. This is because the type (and quantity) of carbohydrate present in a food can vary depending on factors such as the variety of a particular fruit or vegetable, the time of year it is picked and how ripe it is. Recipes used in food manufacture and how a food has been processed also affect values. Carbohydrate foods are, therefore, commonly grouped into high, medium and low GI bands, rather than using specific values.

Above: Couscous has a medium-GI value and is a good accompaniment.

GI values

• Glucose has a value of 100, as it is the sugar that other carbohydrates are converted into when they are broken down. All carbohydrates are rated in relation to it.
• High GI (a value above 70) indicates that the food breaks down quickly, producing a rapid rise in blood sugar and insulin levels. Foods in this group include most breads and breakfast cereals, white rice, mashed and baked potatoes, doughnuts, popcorn, pumpkin, swede (rutabaga), parsnips, broad (fava) beans and watermelon.
• Medium GI (a value between 56–69) includes pitta bread, arborio, basmati and brown rice, croissants, pancakes, couscous, boiled new potatoes, carrots, beetroot (beet), pineapple, bananas and dried fruits, such as raisins, currants and sultanas (golden raisins).
• Low GI (a value below 55) indicates that the food breaks down slowly, producing a slow and steady rise in blood sugar and insulin levels. Foods in this group include pulses (peas, beans and lentils), pasta (all types), oats, rye bread and seeded breads, bulgur wheat, corn, sweet potatoes and chocolate.

From GI to GL

Although this analysis provided useful and revolutionary results, it did not tell the whole story, because it only measured the quality of the carbohydrate and did not take into

Below: Both white and wholemeal varieties of bread have high-GI values.

Above: Watermelon is high GI, but low GL, as it is mainly water.

Above: Porridge with fruit makes a good low-GL and low-GI breakfast.

consideration the amount of food or quantity of carbohydrates eaten in a typical portion size. Figures were, therefore, sometimes misleading, because certain foods, such as carrots and watermelon, were calculated to have relatively high-GI values due to their sweetness and so were restricted on the diet.

When one considers a typical portion size, and the fact that most fruit and vegetables are largely comprised of water and fibre, a relatively small amount of usable carbohydrate is eaten, so the true effect on blood sugar levels is different to what the GI value suggests.

Below: Carrots can in fact be eaten freely, following the GL diet.

Pasta on the other hand, was calculated to have a relatively low-GI value and could therefore be eaten regularly, but because it is carbohydrate (starch) dense, it rates much more highly on GL values and should only be eaten in moderation.

How GL values are calculated

GL values are much more realistic and provide a useful guide for successful dieting, which includes carbohydrates as part of a healthy balanced diet. Values are based on the GI figures as a starting point, but this is taken a step further by factoring in the actual amount of carbohydrate present in a typical portion size as a percentage (by dividing by 100). The GL value therefore measures both the quality and quantity of carbohydrate present in a typical portion size of the food.

$$\text{GL value} = \frac{\text{GI value x grams of carbohydrate in an average portion}}{100}$$

Although it is useful to know how values have been calculated, these are not mathematical sums that you need concern yourself with.

Like the GI index, GL values are grouped according to whether they are low, medium or high, and they are often given a colour coding of red for high, yellow for medium and green for low. Values cannot be absolutely precise due to nutritional variation within food varieties, so categorizing foods according to the range they fall in is more broadly accurate.

GL values

Although no carbohydrate foods should be banned while you are on a low-GL diet, try to eat mainly carbohydrates that have a low-GL value, moderate those with a medium GL and restrict foods with a high GL. GL values for individual foods span a lower range than GI values.

Below 10 = low GL
11–19 = medium GL
Above 20 = high GL

All the recipes in this book have been selected on account of their use of low-GL carbohydrates, based on average-sized portions, and low-GL accompaniments are also suggested. We have included approximate GL values for each recipe (excluding the accompaniments) for your added information and guidance.

You should aim for a GL total of 80 or less daily to lose weight.

Which foods to choose

No food is completely banned from the GL diet. You can choose from all the food groups, so it is both a healthy and varied regime. However, depending on their GL value, certain foods can be eaten more freely, while others should only be eaten in moderation. GL values are also based on average-sized portions so although there is no need to weigh or measure foods constantly, remember that portion sizes should be reasonable and not too generous. However, because low-GL foods are filling and satisfying to eat, you'll find that average portion sizes are sufficient. You should not, therefore, feel hungry or need to snack between meals.

Foods you can eat freely

All of the following foods are digested slowly so blood sugar levels are kept on an even keel. By following the basic principles of the diet you can avoid peaks and troughs in energy levels, hunger pangs that trigger indiscriminate snacking on high-fat and high-sugar foods, and look forward to successful dieting and sustained weight loss.

These foods have a GL value of less than 10, for an average-sized portion, and are ranked as low GL.

Beans, peas and lentils These have a low GL and are an excellent source of vegetable protein, valuable fibre, and vitamins and minerals that may be in short supply in a modern fast-food diet. Most varieties are also a good source of both soluble and insoluble fibre. The insoluble type of fibre is important for good digestive health, and the soluble type helps to control blood sugar levels by slowing down the absorption of sugar by the body. It also helps to reduce high blood cholesterol levels.

You can use dried or canned varieties. Both are handy to keep in the store cupboard (pantry), although canned types are often more convenient as they simply need rinsing before using cold or reheated gently to serve hot. Dried beans (but not lentils and split peas) need to be soaked overnight. The cooking time depends on the variety, although using a pressure cooker can speed this up.

All types are great for adding to soups, salads, stuffings and casseroles and can also be used for making dips like hummus. They can also be used

Above (clockwise from top): rolled oats, oatmeal, whole oats and oat bran are all low GL.

to replace some of the meat in stews, pies, bakes and pasta sauces, helping to reduce saturated fat in the diet.

There are many different varieties to choose from including butter (lima), kidney, haricot (navy), cannellini, borlotti, flageolet (small cannellini), pinto, soya and aduki beans, chickpeas, split peas and green, brown and orange lentils and chana dhal (similar to yellow split peas). This group also includes dried broad (fava) beans and mung beans, often used for sprouting.

Peas, beans and lentils partner well with other foods, including meat, fish, poultry and vegetables, and can be flavoured with all kinds of herbs and spices. Haricot beans are used for making canned baked beans and these too have a low GL, but choose varieties with reduced sugar and salt.

Oats Low in fat and high in fibre, oats are an ideal food for a low-GL diet. They can be used in a range of sweet and savoury recipes, and will help to reduce the overall GL value of the dish. Porridge or muesli (granola) makes the ideal low-GL breakfast, providing slow-release carbohydrate that helps to keep you feeling satisfied until lunchtime and thus preventing mid-morning snacking. Choose rolled oats, jumbo oats or oat flakes rather than instant oat cereals,

Below: Low-GL peas, beans and lentils should be eaten regularly.

CHOOSE FIBRE-RICH FOODS

The underlying principle of the GL diet is to slow down digestion and help suppress hunger pangs by choosing foods that are less refined. Unrefined carbohydrate foods, which are close to their natural state, are high in fibre, and as fibre helps to slow down the digestive process these foods are ideal for a low-GL diet. Cooking and processing removes much of the fibre content of refined carbohydrates, so although the food may be quicker to cook and easier to eat, it is also more rapidly digested so has a higher GL than its unrefined equivalent.

which are more processed. Muesli should be unsweetened, with no added sugar, but can include some dried fruits for natural sweetness, as well as nuts and seeds.

It's easy to make your own muesli or granola, using toasted oats and adding your own extras to it. If buying a ready-made variety, check the ingredients' panel for added sugar. Oaty cereal bars should be viewed with caution because although they provide the nutrient value of oats and may also include healthy dried fruits and seeds, they also tend to be high in fat and added sugar, can be highly calorific and are unlikely to fill you up for very long.

Pot barley This contains the complete barley grain with just the tough outer hulls removed. It is rich in both soluble and insoluble fibre, as well as helping to provide protein and valuable minerals. It can be cooked in a similar way to rice as a side dish or used in salads, soups, stews and pilaffs. (Pearl barley is made by milling the whole barley grain to remove the outer bran layer, so much of the fibre and nutrient value is lost. Because it is more refined, it cooks more quickly.) Both pot and pearl barley have a low-GL value. As previously discussed, the reason why different grains vary in their GI (and therefore GL value) is due to the type of carbohydrate they contain.

Bulgur Often described as cracked wheat, bulgur wheat is produced by cooking whole grains of wheat until they crack. It is then dried and ground to a fine, medium or coarse consistency. Bulgur wheat is a staple in the Middle East where it is used for making a popular salad called tabbouleh, and kibbeh, which are like little meatballs. It is quick to cook and makes an excellent alternative to rice or potatoes.

Quinoa This is a small yellowy-brown, South American grain (strictly a seed) that is becoming increasingly popular. Not only is it protein-rich with a low-GL value, but it is also makes an ideal gluten-free alternative to wheat and other grains. It can be cooked just like brown rice in water or stock for 20 minutes, and has a nutty flavour.

Left (clockwise from left): pot barley, barley flakes and pearl barley.

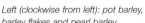

Above: Quinoa is low GL and makes a great alternative to rice.

Fruits Although fruit contains naturally occurring fruit sugar (fructose), this does not give it a high-GL value. Sugar found in fruit induces a slower glycaemic response than added sugar because it first has to be released from the plant cells by digestive enzymes, so it does not raise blood sugar or insulin levels dramatically. The low GL of most fruits is also due to the fact that, relative to its portion size, not a lot of carbohydrate is consumed. Fresh fruit has a high water content and, if the peel is eaten, the fibre value is also high, which helps to slow down digestion. Fruit that is not peeled should be washed before eating to remove any pesticide residues.

Based on GI values alone, certain fruits, such as watermelon, are rated more highly than they are on GL measurements. However, when the quantity of carbohydrate is taken into account, these fruits were found to have a low-GL value, so the fruit can be enjoyed freely.

Bananas also rate moderately high on the GI index. In this case, the GL value is usually rated as medium, as bananas are quite high in carbohydrate. However, since bananas are a nourishing fruit and provide a good source of low-fat energy, you can eat them in moderation as an occasional healthy snack. Choose bananas that are firm and just beginning to turn from green to yellow, as the GL value varies depending on the degree of ripeness. Very ripe, very sweet bananas have a higher GL value than less ripe ones, and so should be avoided.

Above: Fruits in general are low GL and provide vitamin C and other antioxidants and dietary fibre.

The best fruits for keeping blood sugar levels stable include all kinds of berries, cherries, plums, all varieties of melon, citrus fruits, apples and pears. They all have a low-GL value and you can eat them as frequently as you wish.

Dried fruits are a naturally much more concentrated source of carbohydrate, so although they are good, healthy foods, they should not be eaten too freely. Compared with fresh fruits by weight, they have a higher GL value and their high calorie value could impede weight loss. Dried apricots make a good GL choice, whereas dates have a much higher value.

If buying canned fruit, choose those packed in natural juice and not in sugar syrup as this increases the GL value. Similarly, fruit cooked with sugar has a higher GL than unsweetened fruit.

Fruit juices do not include the fibre value of whole fruit so although one glass of juice a day is fine, they should not be a substitute for the real thing. Whole fruit juices with 'bits' have a lower GL than plain juices as they include some of the fibre value.

Right: Salad vegetables are very low in carbohydrate and can be eaten freely.

Vegetables All vegetables have a low-GL value with the exception of a few particularly starchy ones like potatoes, parsnips, yams and sweet potatoes, which have a medium GL and should be eaten in moderation. Sweet potatoes do, however, have a slightly lower GL value than regular potatoes and provide a delicious alternative. Carrots are frequently used as a good example of a food that rates significantly differently on GI and GL tables. Although carrots rank as a medium GI food, they are in fact low GL when the quantity of usable carbohydrate present in a typical portion size is taken into account.

Pumpkin, swede (rutabaga) and broad (fava) beans are further examples of vegetables with a high GI but a low GL per portion.

Do not peel vegetables if the skin is edible, as the peel provides valuable fibre. Wash, and scrub if necessary.

FIVE A DAY
Healthy eating guidelines recommend that we eat at least five portions of fruit and vegetables daily. This excludes potatoes, which count as a carbohydrate. Fruit and vegetables provide protective vitamins and minerals as well as fibre, which helps prevent constipation and other bowel problems.

In the longer-term, eating more fruit and vegetables may help to reduce the risk of two of the main killer diseases in the western world – heart disease and some cancers. As nearly all fruit and vegetables are low GL and can be eaten freely, it is easy to ensure your daily quota is included in this diet regime. Fruit and vegetables should be eaten raw or lightly cooked to preserve and maximize their vitamin value. Cooking water makes a nourishing and flavoursome stock. Juice counts as only one of your five portions.

Below: Choose low-fat dairy products. Cream and crème frâiche have a low-GL value, but are high in fat. Yogurt is a lower-fat option.

Milk and yogurt These contain a small amount of carbohydrate in the form of milk sugar (lactose), so they are included in GI and GL tables. However, because this quantity of carbohydrate is very small, the GL value is very low. Milk is, in fact, mainly water. You can, therefore, have milk in hot drinks, on porridge, muesli (granola) and wholewheat cereals (occasionally) and use it in cooking, but choose skimmed or semi-skimmed (low-fat) varieties, which are lower in fat than full-fat (whole) milk.

Yogurt is fine too, but go for natural (plain) yogurt and add your own fruit rather than choosing sweetened varieties. Also watch the nutrient content of low-fat yogurts because although they are low in fat, they frequently include a considerable amount of sugar. Bio-yogurt has the added benefit of specific strains of beneficial bacteria that help to redress the natural balance of the gut flora and promote a healthy digestive system. If you are intolerant of dairy products or simply prefer alternatives, unsweetened soya milks and yogurts, fortified with calcium, also make good choices.

Cream and crème frâiche also have low-GI and GL values and because they are very low in carbohydrate, they are sometimes allowed fairly freely in popular diets based on a high protein, low carbohydrate regime. However, it's important for successful dieting and weight control also to restrict fat intake. Cream, especially double (heavy) and clotted cream, is high in saturated fat, which we are advised to cut down on, so intake should be limited, although the GL value is low. Further explanation of the fat factor is discussed in greater detail later.

Nuts and seeds A nourishing food choice, nuts have a low-GL value and provide protein as well as valuable vitamins, minerals and essential fatty acids. Choose unsalted nuts to avoid adding unnecessary salt to your diet. Nuts are useful for cooking and in salads, and make a good snack food, in preference to sugary snacks like sweets (candies) and biscuits (cookies), which have a high glycaemic response. However, although unsalted nuts are good for you, they are very high in calories because of their fat content. This fat is the unsaturated type, but it is still very calorific so you should limit your intake.

Right: Unsalted nuts are low GL, but they should be eaten only occasionally, in moderation, since they are high in calories.

Seeds are also low GL and make a nourishing snack food. Include a mixture of sunflower, pumpkin, sesame, poppy and linseeds (flaxseeds) in your diet. They are ideal for sprinkling on soups, salads, stir-fries and vegetable dishes and can also be added to muesli (granola) and smoothies. Seeds also help to lower the overall GL value of a dish or meal, by slowing down the rate at which the carbohydrates are converted to blood sugar. This is why seeded bread has a lower GL value than regular bread. Seeds are bursting with health-giving properties, providing B-group vitamins and vitamin E, minerals such as iron, zinc, potassium and selenium, and omega-3 and omega-6 fatty acids.

Above: Pumpkin seeds are rich in minerals and taste delicious.

Foods to eat in moderation

These are foods that are commonly omitted on low-carbohydrate, high-protein diets, but banning them completely limits food intake and spoils the enjoyment of meals, making it very difficult to stick to such a diet. There is also considerable evidence to suggest that severely restricting starchy carbohydrates in the diet can increase the risk of heart disease, strokes, obesity, cancer and bowel disorders.

Although these carbohydrate foods have moderate to high GL values, (based on average portion sizes) there is considerable variation in GL values depending on the type of carbohydrate, the degree of processing and methods of cooking. So, within these food groups there are good and better GL choices you can make. Good choices have a medium-GL value of 11–19 for an average-sized portion. Others creep into the high GL range of more than 20 and should be eaten only occasionally and in small quantities.

Potatoes Starchy vegetables, like potatoes, vary in their GL value depending on the season and how they are prepared and cooked. For example, new potatoes boiled in their skins have a lower GL value than baked main crop potatoes, and mashed potatoes have a higher GL value than boiled potatoes. All processed potato products, such as hash browns, croquettes and chips (French fries) have a high-GL value as they are more easily digested, and are best avoided. The best potato choice, therefore, is new potatoes, especially the baby, new season variety, boiled in their skins. Just ensure that they are not loaded with butter, which will push up their fat and calorie value.

Above: Wholegrain basmati rice has a moderate-GL value and is high in fibre.

Pasta Although pasta has a fairly low GI, its GL value is moderately high when portion size is included in the evaluation because it is carbohydrate dense. Gluten-free corn and rice pastas, similarly, have a high-GL value. However, when served with a low-GL sauce or other low-GL ingredients, such as vegetables, the total GL value for a meal is reasonable. Pasta also makes a good low-fat choice for a meal, provided that it is not served with a rich or creamy sauce.

Although white and wholewheat pastas have a similar GL value, you should choose wholewheat varieties because they are higher in fibre and therefore aid a healthy digestion. It's also been shown that if pasta is cooked until just *al dente* so that it still retains a slight bite, the GL value is lower than if it is cooked until soft.

Below: Cook potatoes in their skins wherever possible.

Rice Generically, rice has a moderate to high-GL value, although there is considerable variation between different types of rice, depending on the starch content. American white rice and easy-cook varieties that have been refined for speed of cooking have the highest GL, then next down the table is risotto rice. Wild rice and basmati rice have lower values and should just be lightly steamed or boiled. Wild rice is in fact not rice at all but a type of grass. It has a higher protein content than other rices as well as a distinctive flavour and texture. It is often sold ready mixed with basmati rice.

Wholegrain rice also has a high GL but its fibre content makes it a more nourishing choice than refined, long-grain white rice. Basmati rice is also sold in a wholegrain form and makes a good moderate-GL choice. The same is true for Camargue red rice, a wholegrain rice with a red outer skin from southern France. It has a slightly chewy texture and a great nutty flavour.

Rice can be eaten in moderation on a GL diet, but vary it with other grains such as couscous, bulgur wheat, pot or pearl barley and quinoa, which have proportionally lower GL values than the same weight of rice, and serve a larger portion of vegetables or salad in preference to a large helping of rice. Allow no more than 30ml/2 tbsp cooked rice per serving. Like pasta, over-cooking rice breaks down the starches and can increase the GL value further so make sure it is cooked until just tender.

Bread Varieties of bread that are made from wheat flour generally have a high-GL value although there is considerable variation in their glycaemic response depending on the type of bread. Pitta bread, for example, has only a medium GL, but baguettes, bagels and ciabatta are all high. Both white and wholemeal (whole-wheat) bread, surprisingly, have a relatively high GL although wholemeal does make a better nutritional choice. Go for 'stoneground' if possible as it is made with flour that is less finely ground.

Seeded wholegrain or multigrain bread is better as the seeds help to slow digestion as well as providing valuable vitamins and minerals. Pumpernickel or rye bread also has a lower GL value than bread made from wheat flour. Allow yourself no more than 1–2 slices daily and ideally choose one of the tasty, visibly seeded varieties.

Many people are intolerant to wheat as it can cause uncomfortable bloating and weight gain. If you think that you are affected, choose bread that is not made from wheat flour or omit bread temporarily from your diet.

Couscous This is the staple food in many North African countries. It is most commonly made from wheat semolina, but you can also buy barley couscous in health food shops, ethnic stores and some supermarkets. It is quick to prepare, only requiring soaking or steaming, and can be served as a simple accompaniment or used in salads. Couscous has a moderate-GL value, although it is important to stick to an average portion size.

Breakfast cereals Most store-bought breakfast cereals, apart from oats, have a relatively high-GL value as they are made from processed grains – mainly wheat, corn and rice – and usually contain quite a lot of sugar. The best choices are unsweetened or low-sugar wholegrain varieties, which help to add fibre to the diet. Serve with skimmed or semi-skimmed (low-fat) milk and top with seasonal fresh fruit to lower the overall GL value.

Below: Chocolate is low GI but medium GL and it is very high in calories, so eat it sparingly.

Foods to restrict

These are the foods with relatively high-GL values, which can have a dramatic effect on blood glucose levels, causing peaks and troughs in energy levels and frequent hunger pangs. These foods should be strictly limited in order to lose weight, and then maintain a healthy weight by controlling appetite.

Sugar Ordinary white sugar is a highly refined carbohydrate. It is often described as providing empty calories because it provides no fibre, vitamins or minerals and is a largely unnecessary source of energy. However, small amounts of sugar add a pleasant sweetness to foods that would otherwise taste sour or sharp, so a little when really needed is acceptable.

Sugar in hot drinks can soon mount up if you consume a number of cups a day, so try to wean yourself off sugar and retrain your palate by gradually reducing the amount you add. Avoid sugary drinks and drink water instead. If you do have a sweet tooth, choose fruit-based desserts, which satisfy the desire for something sweet while providing valuable vitamins, minerals and fibre.

Fructose, available from most supermarkets, makes a good alternative sweetener to regular table sugar. It has a lower GL value so doesn't have the same dramatic effect on blood sugar levels, and because it is sweeter, you need less.

Pastries, cakes and biscuits (cookies) These foods are made from flour, which has a high-GL value. They are highly refined carbohydrates with little fibre and also generally include a significant amount of sugar and fat, especially unhealthy hydrogenated or trans fats. These are highly calorific processed foods that we tend to eat too much of and which can frequently contribute to weight gain. They provide instant but not lasting energy, so it is all too easy to over-indulge.

Above: Refined carbohydrates such as cakes and cookies have a high GL.

These foods should, therefore, be eaten only occasionally as special treats. Choose healthier options, such as carrot or banana cake, dried fruit biscuits (cookies) and rough oatcakes instead, although even these healthier choices must be limited if you want to lose weight, as they are high in calories.

Chocolate and sweets (candies) A good example of how one needs to consider the whole nutrient value of a food if you are weight-watching is chocolate. Plain (semisweet) and milk chocolate have a low-GI and a medium-GL value because they are high in fat as well as sugar. So although chocolate is quite satisfying to eat, the sugar and fat together add up to give a high calorie value – in fact a whopping 130kcals for just 25g/1oz of chocolate!

When you consider how easy it is to eat a small bar of chocolate, it becomes apparent how easily weight can pile on. The best chocolate choice, is one with at least 70 per cent cocoa solids as it contains less sugar and has a wonderfully intense flavour. Treat yourself to just a little occasionally.

Sweets (candies) are also very high in sugar and most varieties have a high GL so should be avoided. Choose fruit as a sweet treat instead.

How to combine foods

It is generally suggested that the total daily glycaemic load should amount to less than 80 if you are trying to lose weight. This is a total value of the combination of eating a variety of carbohydrate foods.

However, although the GL diet is a sound basis for successful slimming, one needs to consider the total diet, not only to achieve a healthy balance of nutrients but also to make sure that calorie intake is not excessive. You can't rely on GL values alone in order to lose weight, because if you also eat large quantities of fat and protein you will not become slimmer or healthier. The GL diet should also, therefore, encompass a balanced, low-fat approach to eating.

Above: Aim to eat oily fish at least once a week.

Combining carbohydrates

We now know that different carbohydrates vary in their glycaemic response, so a healthy diet should be based mainly on carbohydrate foods with a low- to medium-GL value. However, carbohydrates with higher GL values needn't be banned, because if they are combined with low-GL foods in a meal, the overall GL value balances out to a reasonable level. In addition to this, if your diet is based on eating mainly lower GL carbohydrates, the

Below: The GL value of potatoes can be high, but they can be eaten in combination with low-GL foods.

higher GL ones can also be included, if eaten occasionally in small quantities. Here are some examples:

• Baked beans on toast make a very acceptable GL diet meal. The bread for the toast has a high GL, but the beans are low GL, so together they combine to make a medium-GL meal that is both nourishing and satisfying to eat and helps to keep blood sugar levels stable. Choose wholegrain bread, ideally seeded, and baked beans with reduced sugar and salt.

• Baked potatoes have a high-GL value but, served with a low-GL topping such as hummus, vegetable curry, chilli or salad, the total GL value for the meal is well within recommended GL limits.

• A bowl of porridge, made with skimmed or semi-skimmed (low-fat) milk can be sweetened with a small amount of sugar or honey since oats have a low GL, and just a little high-GL sugar will not cause blood sugar levels to soar.

The fat factor

Fat is the most calorific nutrient, providing more than twice the calories as an equal weight of dietary protein or carbohydrate. Fats are a much more concentrated source of energy than carbohydrates, but

because energy from carbohydrates is readily converted into glucose, much of the energy from fats tends to be stored as a reserve supply.

Meat, dairy products (such as cheese) and oils are the main sources of fat in the diet. This is largely visible fat, such as butter, margarine and fat on meat, but there is also a good deal of hidden fat in our diets, such as in cakes, biscuits (cookies), crisps (US potato chips), pastries, ready meals, fried foods and chocolate.

Most of us eat too much fat, especially the saturated type found in animal products. This is linked with raised cholesterol levels, and healthy eating guidelines recommend that we reduce total fat intake, particularly the saturated type, to help protect against heart disease.

There is also concern about levels of hydrogenated or 'trans fats' which are found mainly in processed foods, such as biscuits (cookies), cakes, pies, margarines and spreads. These are produced by the process of converting vegetable oils into solid fats by adding hydrogen (hydrogenation), which changes the chemical structure of some of the fatty acids. Hydrogenated fats are believed to have the same, if not more, harmful effects as saturated fats and should be strictly limited.

SUGGESTED PORTION SIZES
- Lean meat or skinless poultry: 100g/3¾oz raw weight
- White or oily fish: 125–150g/ 4¼–5oz raw weight
- Eggs: 1–2 medium-sized
- Cheese: 25g/1oz
- Fresh fruits and vegetables (excluding potatoes): 75g/3oz
- Leafy greens and salad vegetables: unlimited, but watch the calorie value of dressings
- New potatoes: 100g/3¾oz
- Peas, beans and lentils: about 150g/5oz cooked weight
- Pasta (as an accompaniment): 50g/2oz dry weight
- Pasta (as a main course): 90g/3½oz dry weight
- Basmati rice: 2 tbsp/30ml dry weight

Nuts and seeds are also high in fat, although it is the healthier unsaturated type, and they also provide valuable vitamins, minerals and essential fatty acids. Omega-3 fatty acids, found in oily fish, walnuts and some vegetable oils, appear to help prevent blood clotting and protect against the risk of coronary heart disease and stroke.

So, although you should limit your fat intake to control calorie intake, some fat is important for a balanced diet. It also makes food satisfying to eat and helps to slow down the digestion of carbohydrates, thus reducing the effects of high-GL foods on blood sugar levels.

Good sources of protein

Protein is necessary for the growth and repair of all the cells in the body and for the production of enzymes, antibodies and hormones, so we need a regular intake. Animal sources include meat, poultry, fish, eggs, milk and dairy products, but plant foods are also valuable sources, especially dried beans, peas and lentils, nuts, tofu (made from soya beans) and Quorn (mycoprotein made from a type of mushroom). In fact nearly all the foods we eat contain some protein. Bread,

pasta, rice, oats and other cereals all make a contribution, so we are very unlikely to be deficient in this nutrient.

Protein from animal sources may also be high in saturated fat, so you should ideally choose lean meat, skinless poultry, and fish. Milk should be skimmed or semi-skimmed (low-fat), and moderate how much cheese and butter you eat. Also choose more vegetable protein foods to replace some animal protein in your diet.

Like fats, proteins help to slow the digestion of carbohydrates. So, when the effect of a meal is analysed, eating a high protein food such as grilled (broiled) fish or chicken, with potatoes, rice or pasta served as an accompaniment, will slow down the glycaemic response of these medium/high-GL carbohydrate foods.

Foods should not, therefore, be viewed in isolation, as they affect one another in the digestion process and it is the total diet that is important. Healthy eating is a matter of balance and choosing low-fat protein foods to moderate the effects of the higher GL carbohydrate foods.

Portion sizes

GL value calculations are based on the GI index for carbohydrate foods. The GI value is then multiplied by the amount of carbohydrate contained in a portion and divided by 100 to give the GL value. This explains why it is important to eat standard size portions when following the GL diet, as larger helpings of carbohydrate foods will raise their GL values and undermine your diet. It also explains why you can eat a larger portion of a low-GL food, such as oats or beans, but only a smaller portion of high-GL foods. Once portion size is taken into consideration, GL values are shown to be much more accurate than GI values.

A simple visual guide to portion control is to divide a standard-sized plate into quarters. Two quarters should be filled with low-GL vegetables or salad, one quarter should hold a portion of lean protein and the last quarter can be a medium-GL starchy carbohydrate, such as a few new potatoes or a portion of basmati rice. Do not pile the food up, just give yourself reasonable amounts and you will find that your appetite will be satisfied.

Below: Eating protein foods, such as lean meat, fish or shellfish in combination with low-GL carbohydrates will help to slow the glycaemic response.

Getting started

The great advantage of the GL diet, compared to many other diets, is that you can eat a wide variety of foods from all the food groups. It is just a case of getting the balance right and choosing mainly low- or medium-GL carbohydrates that satisfy the appetite and keep blood sugar levels stable. The diet is not about deprivation, but actually eating more of certain foods and less of others. In fact, many people discover, to their amazement, that they can eat far more food on the GL diet than they would do usually.

Strict diets that severely limit food intake and calories often lead to a pattern of yo-yo dieting and can result in a tendency to put on more weight after returning to eating normally. The GL diet ensures that the metabolism works efficiently so that a satisfying quantity of food can be eaten and digested, which will provide all the nutrients the body needs, while

Below: It is important to exercise regularly, as well as to control your diet.

restricting unnecessary calories from high-fat foods and refined carbohydrates. Combined with regular exercise, stored body fat is utilized to help meet energy requirements and excess weight starts to drop off.

The GL diet is not difficult to follow or stick to. It is flexible, appetizing and varied, so getting started is just a matter of making that decision to begin changing your eating habits long term. Unlike many diets, you do not need to choose a 'good' time, free of holidays or social functions, as it will not interfere with your lifestyle. And if you are feeling stressed or fed up, there couldn't be a better time to start than right now. Follow the GL diet and you will soon regain your zest for life and look and feel refreshed and revitalized.

How to adapt your diet

To begin with, it is a good idea to keep a diary recording everything, and that means EVERYTHING, that you eat and drink and noting weak moments or triggers that lead to indiscriminate snacking or over-indulgence. A written journal makes it easier to spot unhealthy choices and bad habits, and helps to focus your mind on where improvements could be made. You can then make specific changes that are realistic and achievable. Again it helps you to be resolute if you jot down these diet and lifestyle changes as a list of goals. If you have only vague intentions then it is far harder to put them into practice. Here are some general guidelines to help you make healthy GL choices and to keep temptation at bay.

- Organize store cupboards (pantries), the refrigerator and freezer so that they are well stocked with healthy basics. Clear out unwanted items.
- Carefully plan all your meals and food shopping so that you do not resort to impulse buys that may be high in fat and sugar.
- Choose wholegrain varieties of pasta, bread (ideally rye, multigrain or seeded) and cereals.

Above: Keeping a written record of everything you eat helps to focus your mind and stick to your diet plan.

- Do not buy ready-meals (TV dinners) and foods that are highly processed.
- Choose fresh, seasonal produce.
- Always have plenty of fruit and vegetables readily available.
- Do not skip meals and always eat a good breakfast.
- Be adventurous with new foods that you have not tasted or cooked before.
- Wean yourself off added sugar.
- Cut back on caffeinated drinks and drink more water.
- Allow yourself occasional treats and do not worry too much if you suffer the odd setback.

Free foods

Eat as much as you like of these foods. They are all have a low GL and are low calorie:

- Berries (blackberries, blueberries, raspberries or strawberries).
- Tomatoes and tomato juice.
- Grapefruit (unsweetened).
- Cherries.
- Plums.
- Watercress, spinach and other salad leaves.
- Broccoli, cabbage, leeks, onions (not fried).
- Raw vegetable crudités, such as carrots, celery, red (bell) pepper, cucumber, radish and mushrooms.

Above: Look forward to viewing yourself in a full-length mirror.

Setting targets

We generally know if we are overweight simply because our clothes feel tight or do not fit any longer. Physical exertion may be difficult, or maybe you are uncomfortable with what you see when you look in a full-length mirror.

You can decide how much weight you need to lose by checking height and weight charts, or maybe your general practitioner will have suggested a target weight loss. However, the most common method used for working out whether an individual is overweight or not is by measuring BMI, which stands for Body Mass Index. This is a simple metric calculation that assesses body weight in relation to height (without shoes).

The result of this formula can then be checked against a chart to see whether you are underweight, normal weight or overweight for your height. It is a useful guide to assessing health risk.

$$BMI = \frac{weight\ (kilograms)}{height\ (metres)^2}$$

BMI under 19: underweight.
BMI 19–25: ideal weight.
BMI 25–30: overweight.
　　You should try to reduce weight.
BMI 30–40: obese.
　　Reducing weight is recommended as your health is at risk.

BMI over 40: morbidly obese.
　　Very important to lose weight.
　　There is a high risk of weight-related health problems and early death.

For example:
Weight = 70kg
Height = 1.6m
$$BMI = \frac{70kg}{1.6m \times 1.6m} = 27.34\ indicates\ slightly\ overweight$$

Excess weight does not pile on overnight. It is a gradual build up of surplus energy stored as body fat over a period of time, so it is unrealistic to expect to lose it quickly. For weight loss to be sustained, it should be gradual and steady – about a kilogram (2lb) a week is recommended.

When dieting, it is a good idea to have a goal in mind, such as a holiday or special occasion, to provide an

incentive and set a time limit by when you hope to achieve visible results. Sponsorship that raises funds for a charity is another great motivator.

Breaking old habits

To be successful long term, it is important to assess your lifestyle. Do you skip meals because you are too busy to stop and eat? If so, take stock of your priorities. What could be more important than nourishing your body? Plan your time, get organized and learn to say 'no' to tasks that can wait.

Think about ways of relieving stress or boredom, such as taking up a new hobby, and set some time aside each day to relax and pamper yourself. In order to succeed, it is essential to remove old triggers and situations that could upset your resolve and spoil your best intentions.

Body Mass Index Chart

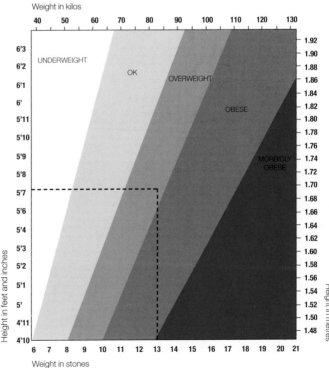

How to follow the plan

The GL diet is not a quick-fix regime or crash diet. It is a lifetime healthy eating plan that will help you to achieve your desired weight and to maintain it. You can increase food quantities after the weight-loss phase but make sure not to slip back into old habits.

Golden rules

Stick to these diet guidelines to retain your new shape and healthy body.

- Eat three meals a day, with low-GL snacks in between if you feel hungry.
- Always eat breakfast – choose from the ideas on pages 24–5.
- Base meals on low-GL carbohydrates combined with low-fat protein foods.
- Eat a wide variety of foods.
- Stick to average-sized portions.
- Choose unprocessed wholefoods.
- Avoid high fat and sugary foods.
- Eat at least five portions of fruit and vegetables a day.
- Restrict alcohol intake.
- Drink plenty of water.
- Keep active and take regular exercise.

Below: The general principles of the GL diet will help all the family to eat healthily.

Coping with family meals

The GL diet is family friendly so everyone can enjoy the same meals. However, for those family members who do not need to lose weight, larger portions of pasta, rice and potatoes can be allowed. They can also eat more bread and puddings. Numerous studies have reported on the benefits of a healthy diet for children in terms of improved behaviour and concentration and preventing obesity, so generally adopting GL guidelines will have a good effect on their nutritional well-being.

Entertaining and eating out

There is no need for this diet to interfere with your social life. Simply follow the same GL principles as for cooking food to eat at home and you will find that you still have plenty of choices.

- Chunky vegetable soups make a good appetizer or light main course. If you do have bread, go for a multigrain or seeded variety – the more texture the better.
- Avoid high-fat dishes, like pastries, rich sauces and fried foods, and anything battered or crumbed.

Above: Vegetable soups make a satisfying and tasty choice.

- Choose plain grilled (broiled), steamed or stir-fried dishes made with lean meat, poultry or fish, or roasts and casseroles, served with a generous helping of vegetables or salad.
- Pizza, risotto and gnocchi are high GL and high calorie, but if you do like a pizza occasionally, choose one topped with plenty of vegetables, chicken, seafood, pineapple or corn, and not one loaded with cheese or pepperoni, which are high in fat. Serve with a side salad.
- Pasta is fine provided it is served with a tomato-based or vegetable sauce that will lower the GL without adding a lot of calories. Avoid rich sauces. Serve with a side salad.
- Main course high-protein salads make a good low-GL choice – just avoid high-calorie dressings.
- If you like Indian cuisine, baked tandoori or tikka dishes (not those in creamy sauces) make good choices or opt for one of the vegetable, bean, chickpea or lentil dishes.
- Vegetarian dishes based on vegetables, beans and brown rice are all naturally low GL but may be high in fat if they include cream or cheese.
- Avoid fried rice and potatoes, but you can have a little plain basmati rice or a few boiled new potatoes.
- If you like a dessert, go for fresh fruit, such as strawberries, or fruit salad, or a small portion of ice cream or sorbet.
- Curb your intake of alcohol and drink plenty of water.

Above: Herbal teas are just some of a variety of caffeine-free drinks available.

Healthy snacks

Traditional snacks like cakes, biscuits (cookies), crisps (US potato chips) and cereal bars have a high GL so are best avoided. Chocolate is only medium GL but it is high in fat and very calorific, so although you can treat yourself to a small amount of good quality chocolate (with a high percentage of cocoa solids) occasionally, it should be eaten in moderation. So as not to be tempted, make sure that you always have alternative healthy choices for weak moments, or for if you are feeling peckish between meals.

Good, low-GL snacks include:

- Unsalted nuts (in moderation, as high in fat and calories).
- Seeds (in moderation).
- Piece of fresh fruit.
- Rough oatcake spread with low-fat cream cheese or peanut butter.
- Yogurt (unsweetened and low-fat).
- Milkshake or smoothie (made with skimmed or semi-skimmed (low-fat) milk or yogurt with fresh fruit or fruit canned in natural juice).
- Dips such as hummus, tzatziki, guacamole or tomato salsa with raw vegetable crudités.
- Handful of cherry tomatoes or olives.
- Mug of home-made chunky vegetable or lentil soup.

Water and other drinks

Experts recommend that we need to drink eight large glasses (about 2 litres/3½ pints) of water a day, and more than this during hot weather or after exercise. Water makes up about 60 per cent of the average adult's body weight but it is lost in sweat and water vapour simply through breathing, so it must be continually replaced. Even small levels of dehydration can cause headaches, poor skin, lethargy and lack of concentration, as well as constipation, urinary tract infections and even high blood cholesterol levels.

The GL diet is high in dietary fibre, which aids healthy digestion and helps to prevent bowel disorders, but it is essential that this material is combined with sufficient fluid intake. Although a small amount of tea and coffee can contribute to your fluid intake, caffeinated drinks act as a diuretic and stimulate urination.

Alcohol has an even stronger diuretic effect and can leave you dehydrated. You can have occasional alcoholic drinks on the GL diet, but remember that alcohol is rapidly absorbed as a source of energy and is high in calories, so regular drinking will slow down your weight loss. A spritzer, made with half wine and half sparkling water, provides a lower-calorie option. Alternatively, a Bloody Mary, made with fresh tomato juice and a shot of vodka, makes a good choice.

Thirst is not a reliable guide to how much water the body needs. The best advice is to get into the habit of drinking water throughout the day, including a glass on rising and a glass before going to bed. This can be bottled still or sparkling mineral water or tap water. For flavour, you could add a slice of lemon or lime or shavings of fresh root ginger, or a splash of elderflower cordial. Soft drinks and juices should be diluted to restrict your sugar intake.

It is also easy to confuse thirst with hunger and to reach for a snack, when really your body needs a drink. Drinking water regularly will also, therefore, help to prevent snacking.

Importance of exercise

Regular exercise is an essential part of any healthy dieting regime and should be part of your daily life. Not only does exercise build stamina, strength and flexibility and improve muscle tone, but it helps to speed up the metabolism, burn extra calories and utilize stored body fat, thus promoting weight loss. It is great for relieving stress and anxiety, triggering the release of endorphins in the brain that make you feel happier, calmer and clear headed. Exercise also boosts the immune system and can help to prevent some forms of cancer, coronary heart disease, high blood pressure and osteoporosis.

Exercise can be anything you enjoy and that you can easily incorporate into your lifestyle. It should be varied and may be a sport, such as tennis, badminton or football, or simply a brisk walk or cycle ride. Many activities, such as dancing or gardening, provide good forms of exercise. You may also like to join an exercise class, but there's no need to take out a gym membership to get fit or lose weight, unless this particularly appeals to you. Ideally you should take some form of exercise daily, and aim to step up your level of activity generally by using stairs rather than lifts (elevators) and escalators, walking instead of using the car or public transport for short journeys and spending less time sitting.

Below: Swimming is a superb exercise to help to tone your body.

Shopping and cooking

Shopping for the GL diet is easy. Supermarkets sell pretty much everything, although you may prefer to use a large store just for basics, then shop for fresh meat, fish and vegetables at individual stores. Open-air markets and farmers' markets are also great places for buying good value, seasonal fruit and vegetables, usually grown locally. There are also pick-your-own farms, which are especially good for summer fruits. Health food stores or co-operatives are also excellent for stocking up on competitively priced wholesome foods like wholegrains, muesli (granola), dried beans and lentils, nuts and seeds.

Checking food labels

Food labels are now very informative and can help you to make healthy choices. Some manufacturers have begun to include GI/GL values on their products, which is useful for the GL dieter, but remember that to achieve weight loss, you must also watch the fat and calorie values of foods.

Below: Ethnic stores and markets widen healthy food choices.

The ingredients panel This is a list of ingredients ordered by weight, starting with the greatest first then following in descending order. This makes it easy to check if a product is high in fat or sugar, as it will be listed near the beginning. There are, however, many different types of sugar that may be used in food manufacture and these may be listed individually, so as well as sugar, honey and syrup, look out for sucrose, glucose, fructose, lactose, maltose and dextrose as they are all types of sugar and their total quantity will indicate the GL value of the product.

The nutrition panel Figures for nutrients can sometimes appear meaningless unless Guideline Daily Amounts (GDAs) are also given. Some manufacturers state high, medium or low against these nutrient values, providing a much more readily comprehensible guide, and a colour-coded system may be introduced in the future for fat, sugar and salt. Nutrient values and energy values (measured in kcals) are generally given per 100g/3¾oz, as well as per serving. Be sure to stick to the recommended serving size if dieting.

GL-LOWERING TIPS
Research has shown that both lemon juice and vinegar help to reduce the GL value of a meal, so sprinkle one or other whenever you can. Here are some suggestions:
• Squeeze a little lemon juice into your morning glass of water.
• Make up salad dressings using just 2–3 parts olive oil to 1 part vinegar or lemon juice. Flavour with crushed garlic, herbs or mustard and seasoning.

• Add a squeeze of lemon juice to soups and curries. It really perks up the flavour.
• Squeeze lemon juice over grilled or baked fish.
• Add a little vinegar (about 15ml/ 1 tbsp) to casseroles. It helps to tenderize meat as well as boost the flavour.
• Sprinkle strawberries with a splash of balsamic vinegar.

As a guide, choose products with:
• Less than 10g/¼oz of sugar per 100g/3¾oz.
• Less than 20g/¾oz of fat (5g/⅛oz of saturated fat) per 100g/3¾oz.
• More than 5g/⅛oz of fibre per 100g/3¾oz.
Watch out for labels that identify foods as being low-fat, low-sugar or high-fibre because although they provide a useful guide, they can also be misleading. For example, many low-fat yogurts are high in sugar, and high-fibre breakfast cereals may also contain a lot of added sugar, so choose carefully.

Choosing unprocessed foods

Carbohydrate foods that are as close as possible to their natural state have the lowest GL. When foods are processed or refined, they are turned into a form that is more readily digested. There is, therefore, less work for the digestive system to do in breaking it down into glucose, so the GL value will be higher. Much of the fibre value is stripped away and nutritive value is lost, although foods may be fortified with added nutrients.

Processing also often adds fats, sugars, salt, and natural and synthetic additives, and these all affect the nutritional value. It is best to choose unprocessed foods or those that are minimally processed to benefit from the full nutritional value and digestive benefits of the whole food. Previous generations used to eat a much more natural diet, before the days of mass food manufacture. Consequently, their diet was a healthier one and, combined with being more active, obesity and the associated health risks were not such a common problem.

Preparation and cooking methods

Any method that breaks down the structure of a food, making it quicker and easier to eat and digest, affects the GI, and consequently the GL value. For example, potatoes that are mashed have a higher GL than boiled potatoes. Fruit that is stewed (especially with added sugar) or puréed has a higher GL than whole fruit, eaten with the skin.

Below: Hold chicken skin with kitchen paper and pull, to remove easily.

A vegetable soup that is chunky has a lower GL value than the same soup that has been puréed. Pasta should be cooked until it is al dente, and basmati rice should be cooked until it is just tender. Raw foods, such as crudités, have a low GL.

Adapting recipes Recipes are flexible, so you can easily substitute ingredients, for instance using a different variety of canned bean in a salad, or by using alternative vegetables in a soup or casserole. It's also easy to lower the GL value of a recipe or meal, simply by adding low-GL ingredients, such as beans, peas, chickpeas, corn, oats, nuts or seeds. If a recipe calls for a mashed vegetable topping, like mashed potato on a shepherd's pie, crush the potatoes instead, or add carrots, swede or sweet potatoes, all of which will lower the GL value.

Ways to reduce fat For the GL diet to be successful, you must also watch your fat intake. Here are some simple ways to cut down the amount of fat:

- Stick to low-fat cooking methods such as boiling, steaming, grilling (broiling), stir-frying, baking, braising and microwaving.
- Use a non-stick pan and do not add fat unless the food starts to stick.
- Eat fish more often, ideally at least twice a week.
- Trim visible fat from red meat and choose extra-lean minced (ground) meat. Turkey and Quorn (mycoprotein) mince make good low-fat choices.
- Remove the skin from poultry. (It can be cooked with the skin on, then removed before eating.)
- Choose skimmed or semi-skimmed (low-fat) milk.
- Restrict your intake of cheese, especially hard varieties like Cheddar, and cream cheese. Use a small amount of mature (sharp) Cheddar or Parmesan for maximum flavour without needing to use very much. Edam, feta and mozzarella are all lower in fat than hard cheeses.
- Use butter and oils sparingly.
- Restrict takeaway (take-out) foods and ready meals (TV dinners).

Above: Fresh seasonal vegetables make a delicious high-fibre, low-GL accompaniment to many dishes.

Ways to increase fibre

- Eat plenty of fruit and vegetables, preferably with the skin, if edible. Wash first.
- Include nuts and seeds in your diet. They are great for sprinkling on salads and stir-fries or for adding to home-made muesli (granola).
- Choose wholegrain pasta, rice, bread and cereals.
- Add pulses (beans, peas and lentils) to soups and casseroles and use for making home-made burgers, rissoles and baked loaves.
- Crushed beans and peas also make a great accompaniment, instead of high GL mashed potatoes.
- Eat more vegetarian dishes, but watch your intake of dairy products, which can be high in fat.
- Peas, baked beans (reduced-sugar) and steamed corn on the cob make easy and convenient high-fibre accompaniments to many dishes.
- Scrub rather than peel potatoes and eat the skin on baked potatoes.
- Serve a side salad with meals that are low in vegetables.
- Include more oats in your diet. They are great for sweet and savoury stuffings, coatings and toppings as well as for making porridge, muesli and granola.

Breakfast and lunch ideas

Many popular breakfast and lunch foods, such as toast, cereals and sandwiches are high-GL carbohydrates. It is, therefore, important to choose carefully on a low-GL diet.

Breakfasts

It may be tempting to skip breakfast when trying to lose weight, especially if you are in a hurry or do not feel very hungry first thing in the morning, but studies show that those who regularly skip breakfast are more likely to be overweight. Breakfast is considered nutritionally to be the most important meal of the day. It kick-starts your metabolism and provides an energy boost, although in keeping with GL principles, this should be a steady release of energy that will help to keep blood sugar levels stable and sustaining you until lunchtime.

A good breakfast also helps you to feel alert and better able to concentrate. Be sure, therefore, to make time for breakfast, even if it means getting up a little earlier, to prevent undesirable snacking that will interfere with your dieting intentions.

Quick weekday breakfasts

Accompany any breakfast with a glass of unsweetened fruit juice, such as cranberry, orange, apple, grapefruit, pineapple or tomato juice. Some juices are now available 'with bits' or with added fibre and these make especially good choices. Fresh grapefruit or grapefruit segments in fruit juice also make a good start to breakfast. It is high in vitamin C and supplies some fibre, and acidic fruits like this are helpful in lowering the GI/GL of a meal. Choose pink or ruby-red varieties, which are naturally sweeter, so there is no need to add sugar.

- No added-sugar muesli or granola with skimmed or semi-skimmed (low-fat) milk. Allow yourself about 50g/2oz of muesli.
- Bowl of porridge made with 25g/1oz traditional porridge oats and 250ml/8fl oz/1cup water, skimmed milk, or semi-skimmed (low-fat) milk.
- Wholegrain cereal (ideally low-sugar or unsweetened) with skimmed or semi-skimmed (low-fat) milk. Allow yourself a 25g/1oz portion of cereal.
- Fruit salad topped with natural (plain) low-fat yogurt and sprinkled with muesli (granola) or sunflower and pumpkin seeds. Use a selection of seasonal fruits or a mixture of fresh and dried fruits, such as prunes with banana and orange segments.
- Lightly stewed apples topped with low-fat yogurt and sprinkled with some oats and chopped nuts.
- Milkshake or smoothie, made using any soft fruits, plus semi-skimmed (low-fat) milk or low-fat yogurt. Add 15ml/1 tbsp rolled oats for a more sustaining drink.
- 1 slice stoneground wholemeal (whole-wheat) toast spread with peanut butter and a glass of semi-skimmed (low-fat) milk.

Above: Whizz up a fruit smoothie in a blender or food processor.

Cooked breakfasts

For a more leisurely start to the weekend, treat yourself to a cooked breakfast. Start with juice or grapefruit. Include one slice of 'good' GL bread if you like.

- 1 poached egg with 1 rasher (strip) of grilled (broiled) lean bacon and grilled tomatoes and/or grilled mushrooms.
- 2 egg omelette, cooked with a knob of butter and filled with smoked salmon. Serve with grilled (broiled) tomatoes.
- Scrambled eggs cooked with diced red (bell) pepper, tomatoes and torn fresh basil leaves.
- Soft-boiled egg with steamed asparagus spears or a slice of wholemeal (whole-wheat) stoneground toast thinly spread with yeast extract.
- 2 grilled (broiled) large flat mushrooms, topped with pieces of grilled bacon and a slice of mozzarella cheese.
- Smoked haddock, poached in a little semi-skimmed (low-fat) milk.
- Smoked haddock kedgeree made with lightly spiced basmati rice tossed with smoked haddock, hard-boiled egg, peas and spring onions (scallions).
- Herrings in oatmeal, fried in a little oil, served with grilled (broiled) tomatoes.
- Grilled (broiled) kippers, sprinkled with some lemon juice.
- 2 grilled (broiled) sausages served with grilled mushrooms, tomatoes and/or 30ml/2 tbsp reduced-sugar baked beans.
- 200g/7oz reduced-sugar baked beans on a slice of wholemeal toast.

Above: Acidic fruits lower the overall GI/GL of a meal.

Lunches

Whether you eat in a staff canteen or restaurant or take a packed lunch with you to work, there are plenty of low-GL choices. For variety and convenience, you can have small portions of bread, pasta, rice or potatoes, but try not to eat these too frequently and go for the lower-GL versions. Be sure that portion sizes for all dishes are moderate.

Restaurant/canteen choices

- Vegetable or bean soup (chunky, not thickened or creamy).
- Slice of melon with prosciutto.
- Steamed asparagus spears, drizzled with a little French dressing.
- Mozzarella and tomato salad.
- Smoked salmon or gravadlax
- Greek salad (made with tomatoes, cucumber, feta cheese and olives).
- Niçoise (tuna) or seafood salad
- Avocado with prawns (shrimp) or smoked salmon.
- Grilled (broiled) fish, chicken or lean steak with fresh vegetables or salad.
- Kebabs with salad.
- Teriyaki salmon.
- Lean stir-fries made with plenty of fresh vegetables.
- Meat, chicken or vegetable curry (not rich or creamy) with a small portion of plain basmati rice. Dhansak curries and dhals include lentils and make a good low-GL choice.
- Falafel in wholemeal (whole-wheat) pitta bread with salad.
- Chicken satay with peanut dip.
- Sausages (good-quality) braised with beans or lentils.
- Meatballs in tomato sauce with a small portion of pasta or rice.

Below: Eggs can be used in many healthy dishes.

Above: Seared tuna steaks with salsa or grilled (broiled) swordfish with salad makes a perfect low-GL dinner.

- Jacket potato topped with beans, ratatouille, vegetable curry or salad. Choose a smaller potato and more topping. Be sure to eat the potato skin for its fibre value.
- Open sandwich on rye bread.

Packed lunches

Choose one of the following, plus a piece of fresh fruit. You could also have a low-fat yogurt.

- Hummus, tzatziki, guacamole or tomato salsa with vegetable crudités and/or small wholemeal pitta bread.
- Salads (lightly tossed in vinaigrette dressing with vinegar or lemon juice)
- Beans or chickpeas with diced (bell) peppers, onions, corn, cooked green beans and cucumber.
- Waldorf salad, made with chopped celery, apple and walnuts combined with mixed leaves.
- Grains (such as cooked bulgur wheat, quinoa, barley or couscous) mixed with diced tomatoes, cucumber, (bell) peppers, grated carrots and spring onions (scallions), or chopped dried apricots, nuts and seeds and lots of chopped fresh herbs.
- Chicken and wholewheat pasta with roasted (bell) peppers, sun-blush tomatoes and green or black olives.

- Flaked tuna or smoked mackerel fillet with diced (bell) peppers, corn and broad (fava) beans or a few boiled new potatoes.
- Prawns (shrimp) with basmati and wild rice, mixed diced (bell) peppers, steamed mangetouts (snow peas) and spring onions (scallions).
- Rye crispbreads or rough oatcakes topped with reduced-fat soft cheese or cottage cheese.
- Chunky soup (packed in a flask, to be heated in a microwave).
- Slice of vegetable frittata with salad.

BREAD CHOICES

You can have bread occasionally but remember that both white and wholemeal (whole-wheat) bread have a high-GL value so restrict your intake and do not have more than 1–2 medium slices (25g/1oz per slice) a day while dieting. Avoid white bread made with refined flour. The best choices are stoneground wholemeal, grainy or seeded breads that are higher in fibre as well as having more texture, or rye breads, such as pumpernickel, which are more slowly digested.

Meal planners (80 GLs or less per day)

WEEK 1	Monday	Tuesday	Wednesday
Breakfast	• Half a fresh grapefruit • Bowl of porridge made with skimmed or semi-skimmed (low-fat) milk	• Fresh fruit salad • 1 slice of lightly toasted seeded bread spread with peanut butter	• Grapefruit salad with minted pomegranate yogurt • Handful of unsalted nuts
Lunch	• Lemony couscous, olive and courgette (zucchini) salad OR spiced mixed vegetable couscous • Leafy side salad • Apple or pear	• Winter farmhouse soup OR other vegetable soup of your choice • Low-fat natural (plain) yogurt with raspberries, strawberries or other seasonal fresh fruit	• Citrus chicken and coleslaw salad OR tandoori, tikka or chicken satay with side salad • Small handful cherry tomatoes
Dinner	• Spicy beef koftas with chickpea purée • Tomato and red onion salad • 1 piece wholemeal (whole-wheat) pitta bread	• Barley risotto with roasted squash and leeks OR Indian rice with tomatoes, spinach and cashew nuts • Large green salad	• Salmon with leeks and (bell) peppers • Steamed green beans • Brown or basmati and wild rice

Thursday	**Friday**	**Saturday**	**Sunday**
• Muesli (granola) (no added-sugar) topped with fresh fruit and low-fat natural (plain) yogurt	• Strawberry and banana smoothie (blend fruit with semi-skimmed (low-fat) milk, yogurt and 1 tbsp oats)	• Glass of fruit juice • Grilled (broiled) kippers or herrings in oatmeal with grilled tomatoes	• Boiled egg • 1 slice of wholemeal (whole-wheat) toast spread with yeast extract

• Red (bell) pepper and spinach frittata OR fresh herb omelette • Corn, tomato and onion side salad • Piece of seasonal fresh fruit	• Vegetable soup with beans and split peas OR Mediterranean vegetable hot-pot • 1 slice of seeded bread or a small bread roll	• Pea and mint omelette OR tzatziki (minted cucumber yogurt) served with raw vegetable cruditées • Large green salad	• Roast chicken • Braised lettuce and peas • Steamed carrots and new potatoes • Oat-topped rhubarb frushie

• Italian sausages with cannellini beans • Steamed or lightly boiled broccoli or spinach	• Duck and broccoli stir-fry • Brown basmati rice • Exotic fruit salad (combine pineapple, mango or papaya and kiwi fruit in apple juice)	• Pork with chickpeas and orange • Quinoa, barley or brown basmati rice • Small portion of vanilla ice cream with mixed berries	• Watermelon and feta cheese salad OR Greek salad (made with feta, tomatoes, cucumber, olives and salad leaves)

WEEK 2	Monday	Tuesday	Wednesday
Breakfast	• Fresh figs with pears • Muesli (granola) (no added sugar) with semi-skimmed (low-fat) milk	• Low-fat yogurt topped with mixed berries OR baked beans (reduced-sugar) on toast	• Glass of fruit juice • Muesli or granola with semi-skimmed (low-fat) milk

Lunch	• White beans with green (bell) pepper in a spicy dressing OR niçoise salad (made with tuna, green beans, tomatoes and olives) • Handful of blueberries	• Green pea, egg and walnut dip • Raw carrot and celery sticks • 2 slices rye bread OR 1 wholemeal (whole-wheat) pitta bread	• Slice of melon • Seared tuna steak with red onion salsa OR grilled (broiled) fish brochettes OR poached salmon with side salad

Dinner	• Chicken and leek soup with prunes and barley • 2 rough oatcakes with 25g/1oz Brie or Camembert	• Tomato soup (not creamy) • Crab and tofu stir-fry OR alternative stir-fry made with chicken or prawns (shrimp) and vegetables • Slice of fresh pineapple	• Grilled halloumi and bean salad OR chicken casserole with vegetables • Steamed or lightly boiled baby new potatoes

Thursday	Friday	Saturday	Sunday
• Fragrant fruit salad • Wholegrain cereal (low-sugar) with semi-skimmed (low-fat) milk	• Glass of fruit juice • Porridge made with semi-skimmed (low-fat) milk topped with fruit and nuts	• Smoked salmon omelette (beat 2 eggs with chopped chives, cook in butter and fill with strips of salmon)	• Half a fresh grapefruit • Grilled (broiled) sausages, tomatoes and mushrooms

• Pasta and chickpea soup OR lentil soup • Low-fat natural (plain) yogurt OR small portion of vanilla ice cream with seasonal fresh fruit	• Pappardelle, sardine and fennel gratin OR a small baked potato topped with beans, vegetables, coleslaw or salad	• Lentil and nut loaf OR a hearty vegetable soup of your choice • Beetroot (beet) and onion salad • Slice of watermelon, or a handful of grapes	• Lamb and carrot casserole with barley • Steamed or stir-fried seasonal greens • Crunchy rolled oat, yogurt and raspberry cranachan

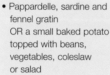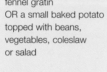

• Cheese-topped roast baby vegetables • Soufflé omelette with strawberries	• Aromatic chickpea and spinach curry • Yogurt raita with walnuts • Poached pears in scented honey syrup	• Chicken and vegetable tagine • Minted peas • Brown basmati rice • Nectarines baked with nuts	• Tortilla with tabbouleh and guacamole OR tortilla filled with vegetable ratatouille and a small amount of grated cheese

soups and light meals

Soups are healthy, versatile and can be made with a wide selection of low-GL ingredients – such as vegetables, beans and lentils – to make deliciously satisfying light meals. In this chapter, you will also find further quick and easy ideas for simple lunches or supper dishes, including an omelette, a vegetarian dip and a bulgur wheat tabbouleh salad, served in a tortilla wrap with guacamole.

Italian bean soup

This satisfying soup is similar to minestrone, but is made with protein-rich beans instead of pasta. You can use either haricot or borlotti beans – both are readily available canned, making this soup very quick and easy to cook. It is then served ladled over lightly cooked fresh young spinach, adding further nutrient value, as well as additional flavour and colour.

Serves 4

45ml/3 tbsp olive oil
2 onions, chopped
2 carrots, sliced
4 garlic cloves, crushed
2 celery sticks, thinly sliced
1 fennel bulb, trimmed and chopped
2 large courgettes (zucchini), thinly sliced
400g/14oz can chopped tomatoes
30ml/2 tbsp home-made or bought pesto
900ml/1½ pints/3¾ cups vegetable stock
400g/14oz can haricot (navy) or borlotti
  beans, rinsed and drained
salt and ground black pepper

For the base
15ml/1 tbsp extra virgin olive oil,
  plus extra for drizzling
450g/1lb fresh young spinach

GL per serving: 5.2

Variation
Other dark greens, such as shredded chard or cabbage, could be used instead of the spinach.

1 Heat the oil in a large pan. Add the chopped onions, carrots, crushed garlic, celery and fennel and fry gently for about 10 minutes.

2 Add the courgettes and fry gently for a further 2 minutes.

3 Stir in the chopped tomatoes with their juice, pesto, stock and beans, and bring to the boil. Lower the heat, cover and simmer gently for 25–30 minutes, until the vegetables are just tender. Season with salt and black pepper to taste.

4 Heat the oil in a frying pan and fry the spinach for 2 minutes, or until just wilted. Spoon the spinach into heated soup bowls, then ladle the soup over the spinach. Just before serving, drizzle with olive oil and sprinkle with ground black pepper.

Energy 331kcal/1380kJ; Protein 15.3g; Carbohydrate 29.8g, of which sugars 14.6g; Fat 17.5g, of which saturates 3.2g; Cholesterol 4mg; Calcium 376mg; Fibre 13.3g; Sodium 621mg; GI 16.5

Lentil soup

This recipe uses brown or green lentils, which retain their shape after cooking. They are very nutritious, providing protein, fibre, B vitamins and iron, and have a low-GL value, making this a very sustaining and healthy meal. Lentils, unlike dried beans, do not need soaking before cooking, so they make an easy option for a quick soup.

Serves 4

275g/10oz/1¼ cups brown or
   green lentils
150ml/¼ pint/⅔ cup extra virgin olive oil
1 onion, thinly sliced
2 garlic cloves, crushed
1 carrot, thinly sliced
400g/14oz can chopped tomatoes
15ml/1 tbsp tomato purée (paste)
2.5ml/½ tsp dried oregano
1 litre/1¾ pints/4 cups hot water
salt and ground black pepper
30ml/2 tbsp roughly chopped fresh herb
   leaves, to garnish

GL per serving: 10.8

1 Rinse the lentils thoroughly, drain, then put them in a large pan with enough cold water to cover. Bring the water to the boil and boil rapidly for 3–4 minutes. Strain, discarding the liquid, and set the lentils aside.

2 Wipe the pan clean and add the extra virgin olive oil. Place over a medium heat until hot and then add the thinly sliced onion and sauté until translucent. Stir in the garlic, then, as soon as it becomes aromatic, return the lentils to the pan. Add the sliced carrot, tomatoes, tomato purée and oregano. Stir in the hot water and a little ground black pepper to taste.

3 Bring the soup to the boil, then lower the heat, cover the pan and cook gently for 20–30 minutes, until the lentils feel soft but have not begun to disintegrate. Season to taste with salt and garnish with the chopped fresh herbs just before serving.

Energy 463kcal/1937kJ; Protein 17.9g; Carbohydrate 40.4g, of which sugars 7.2g; Fat 26.7g, of which saturates 3.9g; Cholesterol 0mg; Calcium 67mg; Fibre 8g; Sodium 33mg; GI 23.6

Pasta and chickpea soup

This simple, country-style soup includes chickpeas and cannellini beans, which are both low-GL foods, and large pasta shells in a tomato and vegetable broth flavoured with fresh rosemary. A sprinkling of Parmesan cheese, or similar, adds extra flavour and appeal.

2 Heat the olive oil in a large pan, add the chopped vegetable mixture and cook over a low heat, stirring frequently, for 5 minutes, or until the vegetables are just beginning to soften.

3 Add the chickpeas and cannellini beans, stir well to mix, then cook for 5 minutes. Stir in the passata and water, then cook, stirring, for 2–3 minutes.

4 Add 475ml/16fl oz/2 cups of the stock and one of the rosemary sprigs. Bring to the boil, cover, then simmer gently for 30 minutes.

Serves 4

1 onion
2 carrots
2 celery sticks
60ml/4 tbsp olive oil
400g/14oz can chickpeas, drained
   and rinsed
200g/7oz can cannellini beans, drained
   and rinsed
150ml/¼ pint/⅔ cup passata (bottled
   strained tomatoes)
120ml/4fl oz/½ cup water
1.5 litres/2½ pints/6¼ cups vegetable stock
2 fresh rosemary sprigs
200g/7oz dried giant conchiglie
salt and ground black pepper
freshly grated Parmesan cheese or premium
   Italian-style vegetarian cheese, to serve

GL per serving: 8.3

1 Roughly chop the onion, carrots and celery sticks, either in a food processor or by hand, using a sharp knife.

Cook's tip
Conchiglie grande are large pasta shells, generally used for stuffing, but also good for satisfying soups. If unavailable, use regular conchiglie.

5 Pour in the remaining stock, add the pasta and bring to the boil, stirring. Lower the heat slightly and simmer for 7–8 minutes or according to the instructions on the packet, until the pasta is *al dente*.

6 Remove the rosemary and taste the soup for seasoning. Serve immediately in warmed bowls, topped with grated cheese and a few rosemary leaves from the remaining rosemary sprig.

Energy 454kcal/1916kJ; Protein 17.3g; Carbohydrate 66.3g, of which sugars 7.7g; Fat 15.2g, of which saturates 2.1g; Cholesterol 0mg; Calcium 105mg; Fibre 9.7g; Sodium 510mg; GI 25.9

Winter farmhouse soup

Root vegetables form the base of this chunky, main-meal soup, with red kidney beans and short-cut macaroni added for extra substance and long-lasting energy. Both swede and turnip have a lower GL value than potatoes, but you can use any seasonal vegetables.

Serves 4

30ml/2 tbsp olive oil
1 onion, roughly chopped
3 carrots, cut into large chunks
200g/7oz turnips, cut into chunks
175g/6oz swede (rutabaga), cut into
　large chunks
400g/14oz can chopped tomatoes
15ml/1 tbsp tomato purée (paste)
5ml/1 tsp dried mixed herbs
5ml/1 tsp dried oregano
50g/2oz dried (bell) peppers (optional)
1.5 litres/2½ pints/6¼ cups vegetable stock
50g/2oz/½ cup dried macaroni
400g/14oz can red kidney beans, drained
　and rinsed
30ml/2 tbsp chopped fresh flat leaf parsley
sea salt and ground black pepper
freshly grated Parmesan cheese or
　premium Italian-style vegetarian cheese,
　to serve

GL per serving: 9.3

1 Heat the olive oil in a large pan, add the onion and cook over a low heat for about 5 minutes until softened.

2 Add the carrot, turnip and swede chunks, tomatoes, tomato purée, dried mixed herbs, dried oregano and dried peppers, if using. Stir in a little salt and plenty of pepper to taste.

3 Pour in the vegetable stock and bring to the boil. Stir well, cover the pan, then lower the heat and simmer gently for 30 minutes, stirring occasionally.

4 Add the pasta to the pan and bring quickly to the boil, stirring. Lower the heat and simmer, uncovered, for about 8 minutes, or according to the instructions on the packet, until the pasta is *al dente*. Stir occasionally.

5 Stir in the kidney beans. Heat through for 2–3 minutes, then remove the pan from the heat and stir in the parsley. Taste the soup for seasoning and adjust as necessary. Serve hot in warmed soup bowls, with grated cheese offered separately.

Energy 257kcal/1081kJ; Protein 10.8g; Carbohydrate 39.7g, of which sugars 15.9g; Fat 7.2g, of which saturates 1.1g; Cholesterol 0mg; Calcium 165mg; Fibre 11.4g; Sodium 436mg; GI 22.1

Vegetable soup with beans and split peas

This hearty, low-GL mixed pulse soup is perfect for satisfying a hungry appetite on a cold winter day. Serve hot, in warmed bowls, with rye or pumpernickel bread on the side.

Serves 6

45ml/3 tbsp small haricot (navy) beans,
   soaked overnight
60ml/4 tbsp green split peas
60ml/4 tbsp yellow split peas
105ml/7 tbsp pearl or pot barley
1 onion, chopped
2 carrots, sliced
3 celery sticks, diced or sliced
200g/7oz new potatoes, peeled and
   cut into chunks
10g/¼oz or 45ml/3 tbsp dried mushrooms
5 garlic cloves, crushed
2 litres/3½ pints/8 cups water
2 vegetable stock (bouillon) cubes
salt and ground black pepper
30–45ml/2–3 tbsp chopped fresh parsley,
   to garnish

GL per serving: 13.9

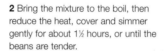

1 Drain and rinse the soaked haricot beans. Put the beans, green and yellow split peas, pearl or barley, onion, carrots, celery, potatoes, mushrooms and garlic in a large pan, then cover with the water.

2 Bring the mixture to the boil, then reduce the heat, cover and simmer gently for about 1½ hours, or until the beans are tender.

3 Crumble the stock cubes into the soup, stir, then taste for seasoning. Ladle into warmed bowls and sprinkle with parsley.

Cook's tip
Do not add the stock cubes until the end of cooking, as the salt will prevent the beans from softening.

Energy 181kcal/769kJ; Protein 8.7g; Carbohydrate 36.9g, of which sugars 3.1g; Fat 0.9g, of which saturates 0.1g; Cholesterol 0mg; Calcium 38mg; Fibre 3.3g; Sodium 29mg; GI 30.4

Chicken and leek soup with prunes and barley

This recipe is based on the traditional Scottish soup, cock-a-leekie. It uses a whole chicken to make a delicious low-GL main-meal soup, but you could add leftover chicken from a roast.

Serves 6

1 chicken, about 2kg/4¼lb
900g/2lb leeks
1 fresh bay leaf
fresh parsley stalks and thyme sprigs
1 large carrot, thickly sliced
2.5 litres/4 pints/10 cups chicken or
    vegetable stock
115g/4oz/generous ½ cup pearl barley
400g/14oz/1¾ cups ready-to-eat prunes
salt and ground black pepper
chopped fresh parsley, to garnish

GL per serving: 11.3

1 Cut the breast portions off the chicken and set aside. Place the remaining carcass in a large pan. Cut half the leeks into 5cm/2in lengths and add to the pan. Tie the bay leaf, parsley and thyme into a bouquet garni and add to the pan with the carrot and the stock. Bring to the boil, then reduce the heat, cover and simmer for 1 hour.

2 Add the chicken breasts and cook for another 30 minutes, until tender. Leave until cool enough to handle, then strain the stock into a bowl.

3 Remove all the chicken meat from the carcass and reserve with the chicken breast meat. Discard all the skin, bones, cooked vegetables and herbs. Skim as much fat as you can from the stock, then return it to the pan.

4 Meanwhile, rinse the pearl barley thoroughly in a sieve (strainer) under cold running water, then cook it in a large pan of boiling water over a medium heat for about 10 minutes. Drain, rinse well again and drain thoroughly.

5 Add the pearl barley to the stock. Bring to the boil over a medium heat, then lower the heat and cook very gently for 15–20 minutes, until the barley is just cooked and tender. Season the soup with 5ml/1 tsp salt and black pepper to taste.

6 Add the prunes. Slice the remaining leeks and add them to the pan. Bring to the boil, then simmer for 10 minutes, or until the leeks are just cooked and the prunes are plump.

7 Slice the chicken breasts and add them to the soup. Slice or cut the remaining chicken meat into neat pieces and add to the soup.

8 Reheat if necessary, then ladle the soup into bowls and sprinkle with chopped parsley.

Energy 343kcal/1457kJ; Protein 37.7g; Carbohydrate 44.4g, of which sugars 27.2g; Fat 2.9g, of which saturates 0.6g; Cholesterol 93mg; Calcium 73mg; Fibre 7.5g; Sodium 95mg; GI 17.1

Pea and mint omelette

Serve this very low-GL omelette with a green salad for a fresh, delicious and fibre-rich lunch or light meal. A tomato salsa or salad would also make an excellent accompaniment. When they are in season, you can use freshly shelled peas instead of frozen ones.

Serves 2

4 eggs
50g/2oz/½ cup frozen peas
30ml/2 tbsp chopped fresh mint
a knob (pat) of butter
salt and ground black pepper

GL per serving: 0.6

Variation
When broad (fava) beans are in season, use them instead of peas. Shell the beans and cook in boiling water for 3–4 minutes. Meanwhile, grill (broil) 3–4 slices of bacon. Add the beans to the egg mixture and crumble the bacon over the omelette when it is almost cooked.

1 Break the eggs into a large bowl and beat with a fork. Season well with salt and pepper, and set aside.

2 Cook the peas in a large pan of boiling water for 3–4 minutes until tender. Drain well in a colander and add to the eggs in the bowl.

3 Stir in the mint and swirl with a spoon until thoroughly combined.

4 Heat the butter in a medium frying pan until foamy. Pour in the egg mixture and cook over a medium heat for 3–4 minutes, drawing in the cooked egg from the edges from time to time, until the mixture is nearly set.

5 Finish off cooking the omelette under a hot grill (broiler) until set and golden. Carefully fold the omelette over, cut it in half and serve immediately.

Energy 205kcal/851kJ; Protein 14.3g; Carbohydrate 2.9g, of which sugars 0.6g; Fat 15.6g, of which saturates 5.8g; Cholesterol 391mg; Calcium 63mg; Fibre 1.2g; Sodium 171mg; GI 48

Red pepper and spinach frittata

This thick vegetable omelette is served flat, rather than rolled or folded, and is more like a cake.
It is packed with colourful low-GL vegetables, and is equally delicious eaten warm or cold.
Serve with a crisp green salad or wrap up a slice to take for a packed lunch.

Serves 3 (cuts into 6 slices)

45ml/3 tbsp pine nuts
30ml/2 tbsp olive oil
1 red (bell) pepper, seeded and diced
2.5–5ml/½–1 tsp ground cumin
3 leeks (about 450g/1lb), thinly sliced
150g/5oz small spinach leaves
5 large (US extra large) eggs
15ml/1 tbsp chopped fresh basil
15ml/1 tbsp chopped fresh flat leaf parsley
50g/2oz/⅔ cup grated Parmesan
  cheese, (optional)
salt and ground black pepper
watercress or salad leaves, to garnish

GL per serving: 0.43

1 First toast the pine nuts in a small,
dry frying pan, taking care not to let
them burn. Set aside.

2 Heat a large frying pan and add the
oil. Add the red pepper and cook over
a medium heat, stirring occasionally, for
6–8 minutes, until soft and beginning to
brown. Add 2.5ml/½ tsp of the cumin
and cook for another 1–2 minutes.

3 Stir in the leeks, then part-cover
the pan and cook gently for about
5 minutes, until the leeks have softened.
Season with salt and black pepper.

4 Add the spinach and cover. Leave
the spinach to wilt in the steam for
3–4 minutes, then stir to mix it into
the vegetables. Add the pine nuts.

5 Beat the eggs with salt, pepper, the
remaining cumin, basil and parsley. Add
to the pan and cook over a gentle heat
until the bottom of the omelette sets
and turns golden brown. Pull the edges
of the omelette away from the sides of
the pan as it cooks and tilt the pan so
that the uncooked egg runs underneath.

6 Preheat the grill (broiler). Sprinkle the
top of the frittata with grated Parmesan,
if using. Flash the frittata under the
hot grill to set the egg on top, but do
not let it become too brown. Cut the
frittata into wedges and serve warm,
garnished with watercress or with a
leafy green salad.

Variations
All kinds of other vegetables can
be added to a frittata. To ring the
changes for other low-GL meals,
add sliced courgettes (zucchini),
mushrooms, corn, tomatoes or
lightly steamed asparagus tips.

Energy 361kcal/1499kJ; Protein 17.3g; Carbohydrate 10.1g, of which sugars 8.7g; Fat 28.4g, of which saturates 4.6g; Cholesterol 317mg; Calcium 189mg; Fibre 6.2g; Sodium 194mg; GI 4.6

Tortilla with tabbouleh and guacamole

Tabbouleh is a classic Middle Eastern salad based on bulgur wheat, which is coarsely ground wheat grains that have been par-boiled. It is quick and easy to prepare and combined with spring onions, cucumber, fresh herbs and a lemon dressing makes a medium-GL filling for tortillas. Avocado guacamole complements the tabbouleh and boosts the nutritional value.

Serves 4

175g/6oz/1 cup bulgur wheat
30ml/2 tbsp chopped fresh mint
30ml/2 tbsp chopped fresh flat leaf parsley
6 spring onions (scallions), sliced
½ cucumber, diced
50ml/2fl oz/¼ cup extra virgin olive oil
juice of 1 large lemon
salt and ground black pepper
4 wheat tortillas, to serve

For the guacamole

1 ripe avocado, stoned (pitted), peeled
    and diced
juice of ½ lemon
½ fresh red chilli, seeded and sliced
1 garlic clove, crushed
1 red (bell) pepper, seeded and finely diced

GL per serving: 12.3

1 To make the tabbouleh, place the bulgur wheat in a large heatproof bowl and pour over enough boiling water to cover the bulgur wheat completely.

2 Leave for 30 minutes until the grains are tender but still retain bite. Most of the water will be absorbed, but drain the grains thoroughly in a sieve (strainer) to remove any excess, then tip into the bowl.

3 Add the mint, parsley, spring onions and cucumber to the bulgur wheat and mix thoroughly. Blend together the olive oil and lemon juice, and pour over the tabbouleh, season to taste and toss well to mix. Chill for 30 minutes to allow the flavours to mingle.

4 To make the guacamole, place the avocado in a bowl and add the lemon juice, chilli and garlic. Season to taste and mash roughly with a fork. Stir in the red pepper.

5 Warm the tortillas in a dry frying pan and serve either flat, folded or filled with the tabbouleh and guacamole, and rolled up.

Cook's tip
The soaking time for bulgur wheat can vary. For the best results, follow the instructions on the packet and taste the grain to check whether it is tender enough.

Energy 303kcal/1275kJ; Protein 8g; Carbohydrate 57.1g, of which sugars 4.1g; Fat 6.1g, of which saturates 1.1g; Cholesterol 0mg; Calcium 106mg; Fibre 3.1g; Sodium 147mg; GI 45.1

Green pea, egg and walnut dip

This mixture of browned onions, chopped vegetables, hard-boiled eggs and walnuts is a vegetarian version of the classic Jewish dish of chopped liver, but is lighter and fresher, and packed with low-GL peas, green beans and nuts. It is also high in protein and the walnuts are rich in essential fatty acids. It makes an ideal light meal when it is served with rye bread.

Serves 6

90ml/6 tbsp/⅓ cup vegetable oil,
   plus extra if necessary
3 onions, chopped
200g/7oz/scant 1¾ cups frozen
   or fresh shelled peas
150g/5oz/1 cup green beans,
   roughly chopped
15 walnuts, shelled (30 halves)
3 hard-boiled eggs, shelled
salt and ground black pepper
slices of rye bread, to serve

GL per serving: 2.6

1 Heat the oil in a pan, add the onions and fry until softened and lightly browned. Add the peas and beans, and season with salt and pepper to taste. Continue to cook until the beans and peas are tender and the beans are no longer bright green.

2 Put the vegetables in a food processor, add the walnuts and eggs and process until the mixture forms a rough paste. Taste for seasoning and, if the mixture seems dry, add a little more oil and mix in thoroughly. Serve with rye bread.

Energy 337kcal/1391kJ; Protein 9.8g; Carbohydrate 11.8g, of which sugars 6.5g; Fat 28.3g, of which saturates 3.3g; Cholesterol 95mg; Calcium 70mg; Fibre 4g; Sodium 39mg; GI 13.6

vegetarian main dishes

These low-GL recipes are packed with vegetables, combined with beans, whole grains, nuts and cheeses to make satisfyingly healthy vegetarian meals. They are inspired by cuisines from around the world, using fragrant herbs and exotic spices to produce an exciting sweet potato, carrot and prune tagine, as well as a lentil and nut loaf and a Mediterranean-style dish of roasted vegetables.

Grilled halloumi and bean salad

Halloumi is hard, white, salty goat's milk cheese that squeaks when you bite it. Here, the grilled cheese is served with baby new potato skewers, and is the perfect complement to the lovely fresh-tasting flavours of the vegetables. The low-GL cheese and the potato kebabs can be chargrilled on a griddle on the stovetop or on a barbecue for *al fresco* eating.

Serves 4

20 baby new potatoes, total weight about 300g/11oz
200g/7oz extra-fine green beans, trimmed
675g/1½lb broad (fava) beans, shelled (shelled weight about 225g/8oz)
200g/7oz halloumi cheese, cut into 5mm/¼in slices
1 garlic clove, crushed to a paste
90ml/6 tbsp/⅓ cup olive oil
5ml/1 tsp cider vinegar or white wine vinegar
15g/½oz/½ cup fresh basil leaves, shredded
45ml/3 tbsp chopped fresh savory (optional)
2 spring onions (scallions), finely sliced
salt and ground black pepper

GL per serving: 5.7

1 Light the barbecue if you are using one. Thread the potatoes on to four metal skewers, and cook them in a large pan of salted boiling water for about 7 minutes, or until almost tender.

2 Add the green beans to the pan and cook for 3 minutes more. Tip in the broad beans and cook for 2 minutes more, then drain all the vegetables in a large colander.

3 Remove the potatoes, still on their skewers, from the colander, then refresh the beans under plenty of cold running water. Pop each broad bean out of its skin to reveal the bright green inner bean. Place the beans in a bowl, cover and set aside.

4 Place the halloumi slices and the potato skewers in a wide dish. Whisk the garlic and oil together with a generous grinding of black pepper. Add to the dish and toss the halloumi and potato skewers in the mixture.

5 Once the flames have died down on the barbecue, rake the coals over to one side. Position a grill rack over the coals to heat.

6 When the coals are hot, heat a griddle until drops of water sprinkled onto the surface evaporate instantly. Alternatively, heat a griddle on the hob (stovetop).

7 Place the skewers and the halloumi on the griddle and cook for about 2 minutes on each side. If they begin to over-char, move the griddle to the cooler side of the grill rack or lower the heat of the hob.

8 Add the vinegar to the oil and garlic remaining in the dish and whisk. Toss in the beans, herbs and spring onions, with the cooked halloumi. Serve immediately with the potato skewers.

Cook's tip
Savory is a very aromatic herb that goes especially well with all kinds of beans. However, if unavailable, use fresh thyme leaves in the dressing.

Energy 482kcal/2014kJ; Protein 25.2g; Carbohydrate 33.8g, of which sugars 4.7g; Fat 28.3g, of which saturates 9.5g; Cholesterol 29mg; Calcium 317mg; Fibre 13.3g; Sodium 223mg; GI 22

Lentil and nut loaf

This nut loaf makes a fabulous low-GL choice for a meal as it is packed with lentils, vegetables, and both walnuts and hazelnuts. It is equally delicious served warm with seasonal vegetables or cold with a salad. For Christmas or a special celebration, serve this with all the trimmings, and garnish with fresh cranberries and flat leaf parsley for a really festive effect.

Serves 6

115g/4oz/½ cup red lentils
115g/4oz/1 cup hazelnuts
115g/4oz/1 cup walnuts
1 large carrot
2 celery sticks
1 large onion
115g/4oz/1½ cups mushrooms
50g/2oz/¼ cup butter, plus extra
   for greasing
10ml/2 tsp mild curry powder
30ml/2 tbsp tomato ketchup
30ml/2 tbsp Worcestershire sauce
1 egg, beaten
5ml/1 tsp salt
60ml/4 tbsp chopped fresh parsley
150ml/¼ pint/⅔ cup water

GL per serving: 3

1 Soak the lentils in cold water for 1 hour. Grind the nuts in a food processor, then place them in a bowl.

2 Preheat the oven to 190°C/375°F/ Gas 5. Roughly chop the carrot, celery, onion and mushrooms, then add to the food processor or blender and process until finely chopped.

3 Heat the butter in a large pan. Add the vegetables and fry gently over a low heat, stirring occasionally, for 5 minutes.

4 Stir in the curry powder and cook for 1 minute more. Remove from the heat and set aside to cool.

5 Drain the lentils and stir them into the ground nuts. Add the vegetables, ketchup, Worcestershire sauce, beaten egg, salt, chopped parsley and water. Mix together to combine thoroughly.

6 Grease a 1kg/2¼lb loaf tin (pan) and line with baking parchment or foil. Press the mixture into the tin.

7 Bake the lentil and nut loaf for 1–1¼ hours, until just firm, covering the top with foil if it starts to burn. Leave to stand for 15 minutes, then turn out and peel off the paper.

Health benefits

Lentils are one of the nutritional wonders as they are high in protein and fibre and low in fat, and are a low-GL starchy carbohydrate. They also provide B vitamins and iron. Lentils generally do not need soaking, but in this recipe they are soaked to soften them before they are baked.

Energy 422kcal/1750kJ; Protein 12.2g; Carbohydrate 19g, of which sugars 7.1g; Fat 33.6g, of which saturates 6.7g; Cholesterol 49mg; Calcium 89mg; Fibre 4.1g; Sodium 225mg; GI 22

Cheese-topped roast baby vegetables

This is a simple way of serving deliciously tender low-GL baby vegetables, including a colourful medley of aubergines, courgettes, baby corn, onions, mushrooms and cherry tomatoes. Roasting them brings out their sweet flavour, and the addition of mozzarella cheese melted over the top makes this a substantial meal that will please the eye as well as the tastebuds.

Serves 4

1kg/2¼lb mixed baby vegetables, such as aubergines (eggplants), onions or shallots, courgettes (zucchini), baby corn and mushrooms
1 red (bell) pepper, seeded and cut into large pieces
2 garlic cloves, finely chopped
30ml/2 tbsp olive oil
30ml/2 tbsp chopped fresh mixed herbs
225g/8oz cherry tomatoes
115g/4oz/1 cup coarsely grated hard mozzarella cheese
salt and ground black pepper
black olives, to serve

GL per serving: 2.9

1 Preheat the oven to 220°C/425°F/ Gas 7. Cut the mixed baby vegetables in half lengthways.

2 Place the halved baby vegetables and pepper pieces in an ovenproof dish. Sprinkle over the garlic, drizzle with the oil and season with salt and ground black pepper, then toss well. Bake for 20 minutes, or until the vegetables are brown at the edges.

3 Remove from the oven and stir in the chopped fresh mixed herbs. Sprinkle the cherry tomatoes over the surface and top with the coarsely grated mozzarella cheese.

4 Return to the oven and bake for 5–10 minutes more until the cheese has melted and is bubbling. Season with extra black pepper, then serve immediately with black olives.

Energy 190kcal/792kJ; Protein 8.6g; Carbohydrate 11.2g, of which sugars 10.3g; Fat 12.7g, of which saturates 5.1g; Cholesterol 17mg; Calcium 140mg; Fibre 6.5g; Sodium 126mg; GI 8.1

Mediterranean vegetable hot-pot

Here's a one-dish meal that is quick to prepare, then can be left to cook in the oven for an easy, flavoursome low-GL family dinner. On its own it is as a complete meal, but it could also be served with grilled chicken or lean meat chops for non-vegetarians, if you like. It includes both beans and potatoes, so no other accompaniment is needed.

Serves 4

60ml/4 tbsp extra virgin olive oil or
   sunflower oil
1 large onion, chopped
2 small or medium aubergines (eggplants),
   cut into small cubes
4 courgettes (zucchini), cut into thick slices
2 red, yellow or green (bell) peppers, seeded
   and chopped
115g/4oz/1 cup fresh or frozen peas
115g/4oz green beans
200g/7oz can flageolet (small cannellini)
   beans, drained and rinsed
450g/1lb new or salad potatoes, scrubbed
   and halved
2.5ml/½ tsp ground cinnamon
2.5ml/½ tsp ground cumin
5ml/1 tsp paprika
4–5 tomatoes, peeled
400g/14oz can chopped tomatoes
30ml/2 tbsp chopped fresh parsley
3–4 garlic cloves, crushed
350ml/12fl oz/1½ cups vegetable stock
salt and ground black pepper
black olives and fresh parsley, to garnish

GL per serving: 1.6

1 Preheat the oven to 190°C/375°F/ Gas 5. Heat 45ml/3 tbsp of the oil in a heavy pan, and cook the onion until golden. Add the aubergines, sauté for 3 minutes, then add the courgettes, peppers, peas, beans and potatoes, and stir in the spices and seasoning. Cook for 3 minutes, stirring constantly.

2 Cut the tomatoes in half and scoop out the seeds (optional). Chop the tomatoes and place them in a bowl.

3 Stir in the canned tomatoes with the chopped fresh parsley, crushed garlic and the remaining olive oil. Spoon the aubergine mixture into a shallow ovenproof dish and level the surface.

4 Pour the stock over the aubergine mixture and then spoon over the prepared tomato mixture.

5 Cover the dish with foil and bake in the oven for 30–45 minutes, until the vegetables are tender. Serve hot, garnished with black olives and chopped fresh parsley.

Energy 433kcal/1821kJ; Protein 20.2g; Carbohydrate 60.2g, of which sugars 18.2g; Fat 14.1g, of which saturates 2.3g; Cholesterol 0mg; Calcium 150mg; Fibre 16.5g; Sodium 41mg; GI 5.6

Butter bean, tomato and olive tagine

The beauty of beans, as well as being low GL and very nourishing, is that they also lend themselves wonderfully to all kinds of flavourings. This north-African inspired stew is flavoured with garlic, fresh ginger, saffron, cinnamon and paprika, and takes its moisture from tomatoes and olive oil. It is hearty enough to be served on its own with some wholegrain bread and a salad.

Serves 4

115g/4oz/⅔ cup butter (lima) beans,
  soaked overnight
45ml/3 tbsp olive oil
1 onion, chopped
2–3 garlic cloves, crushed
25g/1oz fresh root ginger, peeled
  and finely chopped
pinch of saffron threads
16 cherry tomatoes
generous pinch of sugar
handful of fleshy black olives, pitted
5ml/1 tsp ground cinnamon
5ml/1 tsp paprika
small bunch of fresh flat leaf parsley
salt and ground black pepper

GL per serving: 4.0

1 Rinse the beans and place them in a large pan with plenty of water. Bring to the boil and boil for about 10 minutes, and then reduce the heat and simmer gently for 1–1½ hours until tender.

2 Drain the beans in a sieve (strainer) and refresh under cold running water, then drain again.

3 Heat the olive oil in a heavy pan. Add the onion, garlic and ginger, and cook for about 10 minutes, until softened but not browned. Stir in the saffron threads, followed by the cherry tomatoes and a sprinkling of sugar.

4 As the tomatoes begin to soften, stir in the butter beans. When the tomatoes have heated through, stir in the olives, ground cinnamon and paprika. Season to taste and sprinkle over the chopped parsley. Serve immediately.

Cook's tip
You could use two 400g/14oz cans of butter (lima) beans for this tagine.

Energy 140kcal/580kJ; Protein 3.6g; Carbohydrate 9.2g, of which sugars 3g; Fat 10.1g, of which saturates 1.5g; Cholesterol 0mg; Calcium 23mg; Fibre 3.4g; Sodium 496mg; GI 26

Sweet potato, carrot and prune tagine

This vegetable stew has a deliciously sweet flavour that comes from the caramelized vegetables and the prunes. The sweet potatoes and the prunes have moderate-GL values, but this is balanced by the low-GL carrots and button onions in the dish. Serve it with couscous and a green salad that includes some bitter leaves, preferably with a sharp lemon and oil dressing.

Serves 4

45ml/3 tbsp olive oil
a little butter
25 button (pearl) onions, blanched
    and peeled
900g/2lb sweet potatoes, peeled
    and cut into bitesize chunks
2–3 carrots, cut into bitesize chunks
150g/5oz/generous ½ cup ready-to-eat
    pitted prunes
5ml/1 tsp ground cinnamon
2.5ml/½ tsp ground ginger
10ml/2 tsp clear honey
450ml/¾ pint/scant 2 cups vegetable stock
small bunch of fresh coriander (cilantro),
    finely chopped
small bunch of fresh mint, finely chopped
salt and ground black pepper

GL per serving: 30.9

1 Preheat the oven to 200°C/400°F/ Gas 6. Heat the olive oil in a flameproof casserole with the butter and stir in the onions. Cook for about 5 minutes until tender, then remove half of the onions from the pan and set aside.

2 Add the sweet potatoes and carrots to the pan, and cook until they are lightly browned.

3 Stir in the prunes with the cinnamon, ginger and honey, then pour in the stock. Season to taste, cover and transfer to the oven to cook for about 45 minutes.

4 Stir in the reserved onions and bake for a further 10 minutes. Gently stir in the chopped coriander and mint, and serve the tagine immediately.

Health benefits
Sweet potatoes are an excellent source of beta-carotene and they provide good amounts of vitamins C and E. Yams or butternut squash could be used as alternatives.

Energy 388kcal/1638kJ; Protein 5.4g; Carbohydrate 74.8g, of which sugars 37.5g; Fat 9.6g, of which saturates 1.5g; Cholesterol 0mg; Calcium 130mg; Fibre 11g; Sodium 120mg; GI 41.2

Aromatic chickpea and spinach curry

High in fibre, this warming low-GL curry tastes great and boosts vitality with essential vitamins.
Serve it with spicy mango chutney, a cooling mint and yogurt raita, and brown basmati rice.

Serves 4

15ml/1 tbsp sunflower oil
1 large onion, finely chopped
2 garlic cloves, crushed
2.5cm/1in piece of fresh root ginger, chopped
1 green chilli, seeded and finely chopped
30ml/2 tbsp medium curry paste
10ml/2 tsp ground cumin
5ml/1 tsp ground turmeric
225g/8oz can chopped tomatoes
1 green or red (bell) pepper, seeded
  and chopped
300ml/½ pint/1¼ cups vegetable stock
15ml/1 tbsp tomato purée (paste)
450g/1lb fresh spinach
400g/14oz can chickpeas, drained
  and rinsed
45ml/3 tbsp chopped fresh coriander (cilantro)
5ml/1 tsp garam masala (optional)

GL per serving: 5.0

1 Heat the sunflower oil in a large,
heavy pan and cook the chopped
onion, crushed garlic, root ginger
and chilli over a gentle heat for about
5 minutes, or until the onion has
softened, but not browned.

2 Stir in the curry paste, mix thoroughly
and cook for 1 minute, then stir in the
ground cumin and turmeric. Stir to mix
and cook over a low heat for 1 minute
more, taking care it doesn't burn.

3 Add the tomatoes and pepper to
the pan and stir to coat with the spice
mixture. Pour in the stock and stir in
the tomato purée. Bring to the boil,
lower the heat, cover and simmer for
15 minutes.

4 Remove any coarse stalks from
the spinach, then rinse the leaves under
cold running water, drain them and tear
into large pieces. Add to the pan, in
batches, adding a handful more as
each batch wilts.

5 Stir in the chickpeas, cover and cook
gently for 5 minutes more. Add the
chopped fresh coriander and stir well.

6 Spoon into a warmed bowl and
sprinkle with the garam masala, if
using. Serve immediately, garnished
with extra coriander, if you like.

Energy 227kcal/953kJ; Protein 12.7g; Carbohydrate 29.6g, of which sugars 11.9g; Fat 7.2g, of which saturates 0.9g; Cholesterol 0mg; Calcium 285mg; Fibre 9.6g; Sodium 400mg; GI 15.5

Spiced mixed vegetable couscous

This tasty, low-GL vegetarian main course is easy to make and can be prepared with any number of seasonal vegetables such as spinach, peas, or corn. It is ideal for entertaining.

Serves 6

45ml/3 tbsp olive oil
1 large onion, finely chopped
2 garlic cloves, crushed
15ml/1 tbsp tomato purée (paste)
2.5ml/½ tsp ground turmeric
2.5ml/½ tsp cayenne pepper
5ml/1 tsp ground coriander
5ml/1 tsp ground cumin
225g/8oz/1½ cups cauliflower florets
225g/8oz baby carrots, trimmed
1 red (bell) pepper, seeded and diced
225g/8oz courgettes (zucchini), sliced
400g/14oz can chickpeas, drained and rinsed
4 beefsteak tomatoes, skinned and chopped
45ml/3 tbsp chopped fresh coriander (cilantro)
salt and ground black pepper
coriander sprigs, to garnish

For the couscous
2.5ml/½ tsp salt
450g/1lb/2⅔ cups couscous
50g/2oz/¼ cup butter

GL per serving: 5.0

1 Heat 30ml/2 tbsp oil in a large pan, add the onion and garlic and cook until soft and translucent. Stir in the tomato purée, turmeric, cayenne, coriander and cumin. Cook, stirring, for 2 minutes.

2 Add the cauliflower, baby carrots and pepper, with enough water to come halfway up the vegetables. Bring to the boil, then lower the heat, cover and simmer for 10 minutes.

3 Add the courgettes, chickpeas and tomatoes to the pan and cook for 10 minutes. Stir in the fresh coriander and season to taste. Keep hot.

4 To cook the couscous, bring about 475ml/16fl oz/2 cups water to the boil in a large pan. Add the remaining olive oil and the salt. Remove from the heat and add the couscous, stirring. Allow the grains to swell for 2 minutes.

5 Add the butter to the couscous, and heat through gently, stirring to separate the grains.

6 Turn the couscous out on to a warm serving dish, and spoon the cooked vegetables on top, pouring over the cooking liquid. Garnish with coriander and serve immediately.

Energy 572kcal/2397kJ; Protein 21.7g; Carbohydrate 85.6g, of which sugars 14.4g; Fat 18g, of which saturates 5.8g; Cholesterol 18mg; Calcium 198mg; Fibre 11.8g; Sodium 112mg; GI 12.2

Indian rice with tomatoes, spinach and cashew nuts

This tasty rice and vegetable dish is made with brown basmati rice, which has a lower GL value than white long grain rice. It could be served with a selection of other Indian dishes.

Serves 4

30ml/2 tbsp sunflower oil
15ml/1 tbsp ghee or butter
1 large onion, chopped
2 garlic cloves, crushed
3 tomatoes, peeled, seeded and chopped
225g/8oz/generous 1 cup brown
    basmati rice, soaked for a few hours
10ml/2 tsp dhania-jeera powder or
    5ml/1 tsp ground coriander and
    5ml/1 tsp ground cumin
2 carrots, coarsely grated
900ml/1½ pints/3¾ cups vegetable stock
275g/10oz baby spinach leaves, washed
50g/2oz/½ cup unsalted cashew nuts, toasted
salt and ground black pepper

GL per serving: 26

1 Heat the oil and ghee or butter in a flameproof casserole and cook the onion and garlic over a low heat, stirring occasionally, for 4–5 minutes, until soft but not browned.

2 Add the chopped tomatoes and cook for 3–4 minutes, stirring, until some of the moisture has evaporated.

3 Drain the rice, add it to the casserole and cook gently for 1–2 minutes, stirring, until the rice is coated with the tomato and onion mixture.

4 Stir in the dhania-jeera powder or ground coriander and cumin, then add the carrots and season to taste with salt and pepper. Pour in the vegetable stock and stir well to mix.

5 Bring to the boil, then cover tightly and simmer over a very low heat for 20–25 minutes, until the rice is tender, and the stock is nearly all absorbed.

6 Lay the spinach on the surface of the rice, cover again and cook for a further 2–3 minutes, until the spinach has wilted in the steam and all the stock has been absorbed.

7 Fold the spinach gently through the rice. Check the seasoning and adjust as necessary. Transfer to a warm serving dish, sprinkle with cashew nuts and serve immediately.

Energy 421kcal/1753kJ; Protein 10.1g; Carbohydrate 58.6g, of which sugars 10.6g; Fat 16.3g, of which saturates 4.1g; Cholesterol 8mg; Calcium 163mg; Fibre 4.5g; Sodium 176mg; GI 46.5

Barley risotto with roasted squash and leeks

This is more like a pilaff made with slightly chewy, nutty-flavoured barley, than a classic risotto. Sweet leeks and roasted squash are superb with this earthy low-GL grain.

Serves 4

200g/7oz/1 cup pearl or pot barley
1 butternut squash, peeled, seeded and cut
    into chunks
10ml/2 tsp chopped fresh thyme
60ml/4 tbsp olive oil
25g/1oz/2 tbsp butter
4 leeks, cut into fairly thick diagonal slices
2 garlic cloves, finely chopped
175g/6oz/2½ cups chestnut
    mushrooms, sliced
2 carrots, coarsely grated
about 120ml/4fl oz/½ cup vegetable stock
30ml/2 tbsp chopped fresh flat leaf parsley
50g/2oz/⅔ cup Parmesan cheese or premium
    Italian-style vegetarian cheese, shaved
45ml/3 tbsp pumpkin seeds, toasted, or
    chopped walnuts
salt and ground black pepper

GL per serving: 23.7

1 Rinse the barley, then cook it in simmering water, keeping the pan part-covered, for 35–45 minutes, or until tender. Drain. Preheat the oven to 200°C/400°F/Gas 6.

2 Place the squash in a roasting pan with half the thyme. Season with pepper to taste and toss with half the oil. Roast, stirring once, for 35 minutes, until the squash is tender.

3 Heat half the butter with the remaining olive oil in a large frying pan.

4 Cook the leeks and garlic gently for 5 minutes. Add the mushrooms and remaining thyme, then cook until the liquid from the mushrooms evaporates.

5 Stir in the carrots and cook for about 2 minutes, then add the barley and most of the vegetable stock. Season well and part-cover the pan.

6 Cook for a further 5 minutes. Pour in the remaining stock if the mixture seems dry.

7 Stir in the parsley, the remaining butter and half the cheese, then stir in the roasted squash.

8 Season to taste and serve sprinkled with the toasted pumpkin seeds or walnuts and the remaining cheese.

Variation
Make with brown rice or quinoa instead of the barley – cook following the packet instructions and continue from step 2.

Energy 498kcal/2089kJ; Protein 15.6g; Carbohydrate 55.6g, of which sugars 11.2g; Fat 25.2g, of which saturates 5.2g; Cholesterol 13mg; Calcium 287mg; Fibre 7.6g; Sodium 156mg; GI 43.2

fish and shellfish main dishes

Fish and shellfish make a healthy choice for all kinds of tempting low-GL meals. They are a good source of protein and provide many vitamins and minerals. Oily fish also offer beneficial heart-healthy fatty acids. Fish and shellfish is quick to cook, perfect for busy lives, and fabulous for cold or hot dishes, such as hake and potato salad, Moroccan fish tagine or crab and tofu stir-fry.

Hake and potato salad

A 'meaty' white fish, hake is excellent served cold in a salad. Here the delicate flavour of the fish is enhanced with a piquant yogurt and caper dressing to create a delicious low-GL meal.

Serves 4

450g/1lb hake fillets
150ml/¼ pint/⅔ cup fish stock
1 onion, thinly sliced
1 bay leaf
450g/1lb cooked baby new potatoes, halved
1 red (bell) pepper, seeded and diced
115g/4oz/1 cup petits pois (baby peas), cooked
2 spring onions (scallions), sliced
½ cucumber, unpeeled and diced
4 large lollo rosso (red lettuce) leaves
salt and ground black pepper

For the dressing
150ml/¼ pint/⅔ cup Greek (US strained
   plain) yogurt
30ml/2 tbsp olive oil
juice of ½ lemon
15–30ml/1–2 tbsp capers

To garnish
2 hard-boiled eggs, finely chopped
15ml/1 tbsp chopped fresh flat leaf parsley
15ml/1 tbsp finely chopped chives

GL per serving: 10.0

1 Put the hake in a shallow pan with the fish stock, onion slices and bay leaf. Bring to the boil over a medium heat. Lower the heat and poach the fish gently for about 10 minutes, until it flakes easily when tested with the tip of a sharp knife.

2 Leave to cool, then remove and discard the skin and any remaining bones, and flake the flesh.

3 Put the baby new potatoes in a bowl with the red pepper, petits pois, spring onions and cucumber. Gently stir in the flaked hake and season to taste with salt and pepper.

4 Make the dressing by stirring all the ingredients together in a bowl or jug (pitcher). Season and spoon or pour over the salad. Toss gently.

5 Place a lettuce leaf on each plate and spoon the salad over it. Mix the finely chopped hard-boiled eggs for the garnish with the parsley and chives. Sprinkle the mixture over each salad and serve immediately.

Variation
This is equally good made with halibut, monkfish or cod.

Energy 318kcal/1335kJ; Protein 27.8g; Carbohydrate 32.3g, of which sugars 11.7g; Fat 9.6g, of which saturates 1.6g; Cholesterol 26mg; Calcium 134mg; Fibre 4.5g; Sodium 162mg; GI 34.8

Grilled fish brochettes

Serve these delicious very low-GL skewers with aubergine or courgette slices and strips of red peppers, which can be griddled or cooked on the barbecue alongside the fish brochettes.

Serves 4

5 garlic cloves, chopped
2.5ml/½ tsp paprika
2.5ml/½ tsp ground cumin
2.5ml/½tsp salt
2–3 pinches of cayenne pepper
60ml/4 tbsp olive oil
30ml/2 tbsp lemon juice
30ml/2 tbsp chopped fresh coriander
   (cilantro) or parsley
675g/1½lb firm-fleshed white fish fillet,
   such as monkfish, halibut, sea bass,
   or snapper, cut into 2.5–5cm/
   1–2in cubes
3 green (bell) peppers, cut into
   2.5–5cm/1–2in pieces
lemon wedges, to serve

GL per serving: 0.8

1 Put the garlic, paprika, cumin, salt, cayenne pepper, oil, lemon juice and coriander or parsley in a large bowl and mix together. Add the fish and toss to coat completely.

2 Cover with clear film (plastic wrap) and leave to marinate for at least 30 minutes, and preferably 2 hours, at room temperature, or chill overnight.

3 About 40 minutes before you are going to cook the brochettes, light the barbecue. The barbecue is ready when the coals have turned white and grey. Alternatively preheat a griddle on the hob (stovetop) 5 minutes before you are going to cook.

4 Meanwhile, thread the fish cubes and pepper pieces alternately on to wooden or metal skewers. Cook for 2–3 minutes on each side, or until the fish is lightly browned. Serve with lemon wedges.

Cook's tip
Soak wooden skewers in cold water for 30 minutes before using to prevent them from burning.

Energy 260kcal/1089kJ; Protein 28.2g; Carbohydrate 9.5g, of which sugars 9g; Fat 12.4g, of which saturates 1.9g; Cholesterol 24mg; Calcium 45mg; Fibre 2.8g; Sodium 40mg; GI 9.7

Seared tuna steaks with red onion salsa

Red onions are ideal for this salsa, not only for their mild and sweet flavour, but also because they look so appetizing. A leafy salad, pitta bread (ideally wholemeal) and a bowl of thick yogurt flavoured with chopped fresh herbs are good accompaniments to this low-GL dish.

Serves 4

4 tuna steaks, each weighing about
   175–200g/6–7oz
5ml/1 tsp cumin seeds, toasted and crushed
pinch of dried red chilli flakes
grated rind and juice of 1 lime
30–60ml/2–4 tbsp extra virgin olive oil
salt and ground black pepper
lime wedges and fresh coriander (cilantro)
   sprigs, to garnish

For the salsa

1 red onion, finely chopped
200g/7oz red or yellow cherry tomatoes,
   coarsely chopped
1 avocado, peeled, stoned (pitted) and chopped
2 kiwi fruit, peeled and chopped
1 fresh red chilli, seeded and finely chopped
15g/½oz/½ cup fresh coriander
   (cilantro), chopped
6 fresh mint sprigs, leaves only, chopped
5–10ml/1–2 tsp Thai fish sauce
5ml/1 tsp muscovado (molasses) sugar

GL per serving: 1.6

Health benefits
Fresh tuna is an excellent source of high-quality protein, and is packed with nutrients that are essential for good health, including selenium, magnesium, potassium; the B-vitamins niacin, B-1 and B6; and omega-3 fatty acids.

1 Wash the tuna steaks and pat dry with kitchen paper. Sprinkle the steaks with half the crushed, toasted cumin seeds, the dried chilli, salt, pepper and half the lime rind.

2 Rub in 30ml/2 tbsp of the oil over both sides of the fish. Cover with clear film (plastic wrap) and leave to marinate in the refrigerator for at least 30 minutes.

3 Meanwhile, make the salsa. Mix the red onion, tomatoes, avocado, kiwi fruit, fresh chilli, chopped coriander and mint. Add the remaining cumin, the rest of the lime rind and half the lime juice.

4 Season with Thai fish sauce and sugar to taste. Set aside for 15–20 minutes, then add more Thai fish sauce, lime juice and olive oil if required.

5 Heat a ridged, cast–iron griddle pan. Cook the tuna, allowing about 2 minutes on each side for rare tuna or a little longer for a medium result.

6 Serve the tuna steaks garnished with lime wedges and coriander sprigs.

7 Spoon the salsa on to the plates with the tuna and serve immediately.

Energy 628kcal/2608kJ; Protein 35.5g; Carbohydrate 8.3g, of which sugars 7.3g; Fat 50.7g, of which saturates 17.9g; Cholesterol 144mg; Calcium 50mg; Fibre 2.3g; Sodium 789mg; GI 24.2

Grilled mackerel with spicy lentil dhal

Mackerel are delicious oily fish, which are cheap and nutritious. They are complemented by a tart or sour accompaniment, like these tamarind-flavoured lentils. This low-GL meal could be served with a chopped tomato and onion salad and flat bread.

Serves 4

250g/9oz/1 cup red lentils
30ml/2 tbsp sunflower oil
2.5ml/½ tsp each mustard seeds, cumin
   seeds, fennel seeds, and fenugreek or
   cardamom seeds
5ml/1 tsp ground turmeric
3–4 dried red chillies, crumbled
30ml/2 tbsp tamarind paste
5ml/1 tsp soft brown sugar
30ml/2 tbsp chopped fresh
   coriander (cilantro)
4 mackerel or 8 large sardines
salt and ground black pepper
fresh red chilli slices and
   finely chopped coriander (cilantro),
   to garnish

GL per serving: 9.8

1 Rinse the lentils, drain them well and put them in a pan. Pour in 1 litre/ 1¾ pints/4 cups water and bring to the boil. Lower the heat, partially cover the pan and simmer the lentils for about 20–30 minutes, stirring occasionally, until they are tender and soft.

2 Heat the oil in a wok or shallow pan. Add the mustard seeds, then cover and cook for a few seconds, until they pop. Remove the lid, add the rest of the seeds, with the turmeric and chillies, and cook for a few more seconds.

3 Stir in the lentils, with salt to taste. Mix well, then stir in the tamarind paste and sugar. Bring to the boil, then simmer for 10 minutes, until thick. Stir in the chopped fresh coriander.

4 Meanwhile, clean the fish then heat a ridged griddle pan or the grill (broiler) until very hot. Make six diagonal slashes on either side of each fish and remove the head if you like. Season inside and out, then cook for 5–7 minutes on each side, until the skin is crisp. Serve with the warm lentil dhal, and sprinkle with the chilli slices and chopped coriander.

Energy 468kcal/1963kJ; Protein 33.6g; Carbohydrate 35.2g, of which sugars 1.5g; Fat 22.4g, of which saturates 4.1g; Cholesterol 54mg; Calcium 43mg; Fibre 3.1g; Sodium 86mg; GI 28.0

Pappardelle, sardine and fennel gratin

Pasta does have a moderately high-GL value but, combined with the fish and vegetables, balances out to make a dish that is both satisfying and nourishing. Serve with a green salad.

Serves 6

2 fennel bulbs, trimmed
a large pinch of saffron threads
12 sardines, backbones and heads removed
60ml/4 tbsp olive oil
2 shallots, finely chopped
2 garlic cloves, finely chopped
2 fresh red chillies, seeded and
   finely chopped
4 drained canned anchovy fillets, or
   8–12 pitted black olives, chopped
30ml/2 tbsp capers
75g/3oz/1 cup pine nuts
450g/1lb pappardelle
butter, for greasing
30ml/2 tbsp grated Parmesan cheese
salt and ground black pepper

GL per serving: 39.0

1 Preheat the oven to 200°C/400°F/ Gas 6. Cut the fennel bulbs in half and cook them in a pan of lightly salted, boiling water with the saffron threads for about 10 minutes, until tender.

2 Drain, reserving the cooking liquid, and cut into small dice. Then finely chop the sardines, season with salt and pepper and set aside until required.

3 Heat the oil in a pan, add the shallots and garlic, and cook until thay are lightly coloured. Add the chillies and sardines, and cook for 3 minutes. Stir in the fennel and cook for 3 minutes. If the mixture seems dry, add a little of the reserved fennel water.

4 Add the anchovies or olives and cook for 1 minute; stir in the capers and pine nuts, and season. Simmer for 3 minutes more, then turn off the heat.

5 Meanwhile, pour the reserved fennel liquid into a pan and top it up with enough water to cook the pasta. Stir in a little salt, bring to the boil and add the pappardelle. Cook dried pasta for about 12 minutes; fresh pasta until it rises to the surface of the water. When the pasta is just tender, drain it.

6 Grease a shallow ovenproof dish and put in a layer of pasta, then make a layer of the sardine mixture. Continue until all the pasta and sardine mixture has been used, finishing with the fish. Sprinkle over the Parmesan; bake for 15 minutes, until golden brown.

Energy 597kcal/2512kJ; Protein 41.3g; Carbohydrate 57.3g, of which sugars 4.1g; Fat 24.2g, of which saturates 5.4g; Cholesterol 6mg; Calcium 214mg; Fibre 4g; Sodium 303mg; GI 45.6

Moroccan fish tagine with couscous

This colourful fish stew makes an easy yet special low-GL dish for entertaining. Serve with couscous or basmati rice with an exotic fruit salad to follow for dessert.

Serves 8

1.3kg/3lb firm fish fillets such as monkfish or
   hoki, skinned and cut into 5cm/2in cubes
60ml/4 tbsp olive oil
4 onions, chopped
1 large aubergine (eggplant), cut into
   1cm/½in cubes
2 courgettes (zucchini), cut into 1cm/½in dice
400g/14oz can chopped tomatoes
400ml/14fl oz/1⅔ cups passata (bottled
   strained tomatoes)
200ml/7fl oz/scant 1 cup fish stock
1 preserved lemon, chopped
90g/3½oz/scant 1 cup olives
400g/14oz can chickpeas, drained and rinsed
60ml/4 tbsp chopped fresh coriander (cilantro)
salt and ground black pepper
couscous, to serve
coriander sprigs, to garnish

For the harissa
3 large fresh red chillies, seeded and chopped
3 garlic cloves, peeled
15ml/1 tbsp ground coriander
30ml/2 tbsp ground cumin
5ml/1 tsp ground cinnamon
grated rind of 1 lemon
30ml/2 tbsp sunflower oil

GL per serving: 5.0

1 To make the harissa, whizz all of the ingredients in a food processor to a smooth paste.

2 Put the fish in a wide bowl and add 30ml/2 tbsp of the harissa. Toss to coat, cover and chill for at least 1 hour.

3 Heat half the oil in a shallow pan. Cook the onions for about 10 minutes. Stir in the remaining harissa; cook for 5 minutes, stirring occasionally.

4 Heat the remaining oil in a separate pan. Add the aubergine and fry for 10 minutes. Add the courgettes and fry the vegetables for a further 2 minutes.

5 Tip the aubergine mixture into the shallow pan and combine with the onions, then stir in the tomatoes, the passata and stock. Bring to the boil, then lower the heat and simmer the mixture for about 20 minutes.

6 Stir the fish and preserved lemon into the pan. Add the olives and chickpeas, and stir gently. Cover and simmer over a low heat for 15–20 minutes until the fish is just cooked through.

7 Season to taste. Stir in the chopped coriander. Serve with couscous and garnish with coriander sprigs.

Cook's tip
To get ahead, make the harissa in advance and store in a sealed container in the refrigerator.

Energy 338kcal/1422kJ; Protein 33.7g; Carbohydrate 24.7g, of which sugars 12.1g; Fat 12.4g, of which saturates 1.8g; Cholesterol 23mg; Calcium 100mg; Fibre 6.6g; Sodium 517mg; GI 23.3

Salmon with leeks and peppers

Attractive paper parcels of fish are as healthy as they are tasty. The fish and vegetables cook in their own juices, allowing them to retain all their valuable nutrients as well as their flavour and moisture. Serve this low-GL treat with boiled or steamed baby new potatoes.

5 When the vegetable mixture is cool, divide it equally among the parchment or foil and top with a portion of salmon.

6 Drizzle each portion of fish with a little sesame oil and sprinkle with the remaining chives and the chopped fennel fronds. Season with a little more ground black pepper.

7 Fold the baking parchment or foil over to enclose the fish, rolling and twisting the edges together to seal the parcels completely.

8 Place the parcels on a baking sheet and bake for 15–20 minutes, or until the parcels are puffed up and, if made with parchment, lightly browned.

9 Carefully transfer the parcels to six warmed serving plates and serve immediately, still wrapped in baking parchment or foil.

Serves 6

25ml/1½ tbsp vegetable oil
2 yellow (bell) peppers, seeded and
    thinly sliced
4cm/1½in fresh root ginger, peeled and
    finely shredded
1 large fennel bulb, thinly sliced, fronds
    chopped and reserved
1 fresh green chilli, seeded and
    finely shredded
2 large leeks, cut into 10cm/4in lengths
    and shredded lengthways
30ml/2 tbsp chopped fresh chives
10ml/2 tsp light soy sauce
6 portions salmon fillet, each weighing
    about 150–175g/5–6oz, skinned
10ml/2 tsp toasted sesame oil
salt and ground black pepper

GL per serving: 0.6

1 Heat the oil in a large, non-stick frying pan. Add the yellow peppers, ginger and fennel bulb, and cook, stirring occasionally, for 5–6 minutes, until they are softened, but not browned.

2 Add the green chilli and shredded leeks to the pan and cook, stirring occasionally, for about 3 minutes, until the leeks have softened.

3 Stir in half the chopped chives and the soy sauce, and season to taste with a little salt and freshly ground black pepper. Set the vegetable mixture aside to cool slightly.

4 Meanwhile, preheat the oven to 190°C/375°F/Gas 5. Cut six 35cm/14in rounds of baking parchment or foil and set aside.

Energy 268kcal/1118kJ; Protein 25.3g; Carbohydrate 5.9g, of which sugars 5.4g; Fat 16.1g, of which saturates 2.6g; Cholesterol 58mg; Calcium 50mg; Fibre 2.8g; Sodium 178mg; GI 7.3

Crab and tofu stir-fry

For a year-round light meal, this speedy stir-fry makes an ideal choice for a low-GL meal.
Crab meat has a strong flavour so you should only use a little. Fresh crab meat is best but,
if unavailable, the canned variety can be used as a handy store-cupboard alternative.

Serves 2

250g/9oz firm tofu
60ml/4 tbsp vegetable oil
2 garlic cloves, finely chopped
115g/4oz white crab meat
130g/4½oz/generous 1 cup baby corn,
    halved lengthways
2 spring onions (scallions), chopped
1 fresh red chilli, seeded and
    finely chopped
30ml/2 tbsp soy sauce
15ml/1 tbsp Thai fish sauce
5ml/1 tsp light muscovado (brown) sugar
juice of 1 lime
small bunch fresh coriander (cilantro),
    chopped, to garnish
lime wedges, to serve

GL per serving: 5.7

1 Using a sharp knife, cut the tofu into
1cm/½in cubes.

2 Heat the oil in a wok or large, heavy
frying pan. Add the tofu cubes and
stir-fry until golden. Remove the tofu
with a slotted spoon and set aside.

3 Add the garlic to the wok or pan
and stir-fry until golden.

4 Add the crab meat, tofu, corn, spring
onions, chilli, soy sauce, fish sauce and
sugar. Cook, stirring constantly, until the
vegetables are just tender.

5 Stir in the lime juice, sprinkle with
coriander and serve with lime wedges.

Health benefits
Tofu is made from soya beans,
which have the highest nutritional
value of all beans. Tofu is rich in
protein and low in fat and contains
phytoestrogens, hormone-like
chemicals that may help to protect
against certain cancers, heart
disease, osteoporosis and
menopausal symptoms.

Energy 362kcal/1500kJ; Protein 22.8g; Carbohydrate 4.7g, of which sugars 3.8g; Fat 28.1g, of which saturates 3.3g; Cholesterol 41mg; Calcium 719mg; Fibre 1.2g; Sodium 1064mg; GI 37.1

poultry and meat main dishes

Lean meat and poultry dishes provide a great source of protein, iron, zinc and B vitamins, and often form the basis of many family meals. This selection of recipes includes warming stews and casseroles as well as lighter dishes such as chicken salad and spicy beef kofta, all boosted with vegetables, dried beans, peas or wholegrains to produce appetizing low-GL meals.

Citrus chicken and coleslaw salad

This attractive, zesty salad offers a delicious combination of healthy raw vegetables, lean, grilled chicken, and oranges and limes, which are rich in vitamin C. Shredded white cabbage, carrots, celery and spring onions make up the low-GL coleslaw salad, which, together with the fruits, makes a significant contribution to your daily intake of fruit and vegetables.

Serves 4

4 skinless chicken breast portions
4 oranges
5ml/1 tsp Dijon mustard
15ml/1 tbsp clear honey
60ml/4 tbsp extra virgin olive oil
300g/11oz/2¾ cups white cabbage,
   finely shredded
300g/11oz carrots, peeled and thinly sliced
2 spring onions (scallions), thinly sliced
2 celery sticks, cut into matchsticks
30ml/2 tbsp chopped fresh tarragon
2 limes
salt and ground black pepper

GL per serving: 1.7

1 Place the chicken under a preheated grill (broiler) and cook for 5 minutes on each side, or until it is cooked through and golden brown. Leave to cool.

2 Peel two of the oranges, cutting off all pith, then cut out the segments.

3 Grate the rind and squeeze the juice from one of the remaining oranges and place in a large bowl. Stir in the mustard, 5ml/1 tsp of the clear honey, the oil and seasoning and whisk together to combine.

4 Add the shredded cabbage, sliced carrots, spring onions and celery to the bowl, mix well and leave to stand for 10 minutes at room temperature.

5 Meanwhile, squeeze the juice from the remaining orange and mix it in a small bowl with the remaining honey and chopped tarragon.

6 Peel and segment the limes and lightly mix the segments into the tarragon dressing with the reserved orange segments. Season to taste with salt and black pepper.

7 Slice the chicken and stir into the dressing with the oranges and limes. Divide the coleslaw salad among four plates, add the chicken, then serve.

Energy 338kcal/1420kJ; Protein 38.7g; Carbohydrate 17.6g, of which sugars 17.5g; Fat 13g, of which saturates 2g; Cholesterol 105mg; Calcium 112mg; Fibre 4g; Sodium 112mg; GI 6.7

Chicken, split pea and aubergine koresh

This hearty and colourful stew is a Californian version of a traditional Persian recipe. In Iran, lamb is generally the meat of choice, and you could substitute chunks of lean meat for the chicken, if you prefer. Split peas are a nourishing low-GL carbohydrate, making this a very satisfying dish. Serve with a little basmati rice for a healthy main meal.

Serves 4

50g/2oz/¼ cup green or yellow split peas
60ml/4 tbsp olive oil
1 large or 2 small onions, finely chopped
500g/1¼lb boneless chicken
   thighs, skinned
500ml/17fl oz/2¼ cups chicken stock
5ml/1 tsp ground turmeric
2.5ml/½ tsp ground cinnamon
1.5ml/¼ tsp freshly grated nutmeg
2 aubergines (eggplants), diced
8–10 ripe tomatoes, diced
2 garlic cloves, crushed
30ml/2 tbsp fresh mint, chopped
salt and ground black pepper
fresh mint, to garnish

GL per serving: 2.0

1 Put the split peas in a bowl, pour over cold water to cover, then leave to soak for about 4 hours. Drain well.

2 Heat half the oil in a flameproof casserole or a large, deep frying pan. Add two-thirds of the onions and cook for about 5 minutes, until the onions have softened slightly. Add the chicken and cook for 8–10 minutes, until it is golden brown on all sides.

3 Drain the soaked split peas, then add to the chicken mixture with the stock, turmeric, cinnamon and nutmeg.

4 Cover and cook over a medium-low heat for 40 minutes, until the split peas are tender and the chicken is cooked.

5 Heat the remaining oil in a pan, add the aubergines and remaining onions and cook until lightly browned. Add the tomatoes, garlic and mint. Season to taste with salt and black pepper.

6 Just before serving, stir the aubergine mixture into the chicken and split pea stew. Garnish with fresh mint leaves.

Energy 334kcal/1399kJ; Protein 27.7g; Carbohydrate 23.2g, of which sugars 13.3g; Fat 15.2g, of which saturates 2.7g; Cholesterol 105mg; Calcium 87mg; Fibre 5.8g; Sodium 117mg; GI 14.0

Chicken casserole with vegetables

This appealing low-GL casserole of tender chicken, winter root vegetables and lentils, finished with crème fraîche, mustard and tarragon, makes an easy family meal that, once prepared, can be left to simmer gently. Serve with small baked potatoes and seasonal greens. You can cook the chicken with the skin on, but remove it before eating as it is high in fat.

3 Add the onions to the casserole and cook for 5 minutes, stirring, until they begin to soften and colour. Add the leeks, carrots, swede and lentils to the casserole and stir over a medium heat for 2 minutes.

4 Return the chicken to the pan, then add the stock, apple juice and seasoning. Bring to the boil and cover the pan tightly. Cook in the oven for 50–60 minutes, or until the chicken and lentils are tender.

5 Place the casserole on the hob (stovetop) over a medium heat. Lift out the chicken and vegetables on to a plate using a slotted spoon.

6 Stir the crème fraîche, wholegrain mustard and chopped tarragon into the casserole, then simmer gently for about 2 minutes, stirring continuously, until thickened slightly. Taste and readjust the seasoning if necessary.

7 Return the chicken and vegetables to the casserole and heat through in the sauce. Garnish with fresh tarragon sprigs and serve immediately.

Serves 4

350g/12oz onions
350g/12oz leeks
225g/8oz carrots
450g/1lb swede (rutabaga)
30ml/2 tbsp olive oil
4 chicken portions, about 900g/2lb
　total weight
115g/4oz/½ cup green lentils
475ml/16fl oz/2 cups chicken stock
300ml/½ pint/1¼ cups apple juice
45ml/3 tbsp crème fraîche
10ml/2 tsp wholegrain mustard
30ml/2 tbsp chopped fresh tarragon
salt and ground black pepper
fresh tarragon sprigs, to garnish

GL per serving: 4.4

1 Preheat the oven to 190°C/375°F/ Gas 5. Chop all of the vegetables into chunky pieces.

2 Heat the oil in a large flameproof casserole. Season the chicken portions and brown them all over in the hot oil for 5–7 minutes until golden. Remove the chicken from the pan and set aside.

Cook's tip
Chop all the vegetables into similarly sized pieces so that they cook evenly.

Energy 462kcal/1947kJ; Protein 46.9g; Carbohydrate 41.3g, of which sugars 24.5g; Fat 13.4g, of which saturates 4.5g; Cholesterol 118mg; Calcium 156mg; Fibre 9.2g; Sodium 133mg; GI 19.2

Chicken and vegetable tagine

This Moroccan-style, warmly spiced stew is packed with vegetables, including parsnip, turnip, carrots, tomatoes, pepper and green beans, as well as chickpeas and olives – a fabulous low-GL combination. It makes a substantial meal on its own, but it could be served with a little brown rice, couscous or quinoa plus a mixed leaf salad.

Serves 4

4 chicken breast fillets, cut into
   large pieces
30ml/2 tbsp olive oil
1 large onion, chopped
2 garlic cloves, crushed
1 parsnip, cut into cubes
1 turnip, cut into cubes
3 carrots, thickly sliced
4 tomatoes, chopped
1 cinnamon stick
4 cloves
5ml/1 tsp ground ginger
1 bay leaf
1.5–2.5ml/¼–½ tsp cayenne pepper
350ml/12fl oz/1½ cups chicken stock
400g/14oz can chickpeas, drained
   and rinsed
1 red (bell) pepper, seeded and sliced
150g/5oz green beans, halved
1 piece of preserved lemon peel, thinly sliced
20–30 pitted black or green olives
salt

GL per serving: 0.7

1 First skin the chicken breasts. Insert one finger under the skin and grasp it with kitchen paper to prevent it from slipping, then pull the skin away from the meat. Trim off any fat.

2 Heat half the olive oil in a large, flameproof casserole and cook the chicken pieces until evenly browned. Transfer to a plate.

3 Heat the remaining oil and cook the onion, garlic, parsnip, turnip and carrots over a medium heat for 4–5 minutes until lightly browned, stirring frequently. Lower the heat, cover and cook for 5 minutes more, stirring occasionally.

4 Add the tomatoes, cook for a few minutes, then add the cinnamon stick, cloves, ginger, bay leaf and cayenne pepper. Cook for 1–2 minutes.

5 Pour in the chicken stock, add the chickpeas and browned chicken pieces, and season with a little salt. Cover and simmer for 25 minutes.

6 When the vegetables are almost tender, stir in the pepper and green beans, and simmer for 10 minutes. Add the preserved lemon, if using, and the olives, stir well and cook for 5 minutes more.

7 Serve the chicken tagine in the traditional dish, if you have one, or from the casserole used for cooking.

Cook's tip
Wash preserved lemons before cooking to remove excess salt.

Energy 450kcal/1891kJ; Protein 46.9g; Carbohydrate 36.2g, of which sugars 16.4g; Fat 14g, of which saturates 2.3g; Cholesterol 105mg; Calcium 131mg; Fibre 10.8g; Sodium 901mg; GI 7.2

Duck and broccoli stir-fry

Although duck is often considered to be a fatty meat, if the skin and fat are removed, the lean meat is ideal for a Chinese-style stir-fry, producing a low-GL dish with a rich flavour. You could also use skinless, chicken or turkey breast fillets, if you prefer. Broccoli is one of the most nutritious of all vegetables and stir-frying retains the maximum vitamin value.

Serves 4

400g/14oz duck breast
  fillets, skinned
15ml/1 tbsp sesame oil
15ml/1 tbsp vegetable oil
4 garlic cloves, finely sliced
2.5ml/½ tsp dried chilli flakes
15ml/1 tbsp Thai fish sauce
15ml/1 tbsp light soy sauce
120ml/4fl oz/½ cup water
1 large head broccoli, cut into
  small florets
coriander (cilantro) and 15ml/1 tbsp
  toasted sesame seeds, to garnish

GL per serving: 0.3

1 Cut the duck into bitesize pieces. Heat the oils in a wok or large, heavy frying pan and stir-fry the garlic over a medium heat until it is golden brown – do not let it burn. Add the duck to the pan and stir-fry for a further 2 minutes, until the meat begins to brown.

2 Stir in the chilli flakes, fish sauce, soy sauce and water. Add the broccoli and continue to stir-fry for about 2 minutes, until the duck and broccoli are just cooked through.

3 Serve on warmed plates, garnished with coriander and sesame seeds.

Variations
Pak choi (bok choy) or Chinese flowering cabbage can be used instead of broccoli. You could also add some beansprouts or any type of mushroom.

Energy 210kcal/878kJ; Protein 24.8g; Carbohydrate 2.3g, of which sugars 2g; Fat 13g, of which saturates 2.3g; Cholesterol 110mg; Calcium 76mg; Fibre 2.9g; Sodium 386mg; GI 10.0

Pork with chickpeas and orange

This Greek recipe is a wonderful example of how well dried beans or peas, in this case chickpeas, combine with meat in a casserole to produce a satisfying, medium-GL dish. It is also lower in saturated fat than a casserole just made with meat, as protein-rich chickpeas allow for less meat to be used. Packed with flavour, it is guaranteed to please the taste buds.

Serves 4

350g/12oz/1¾ cups dried chickpeas, soaked
   overnight in water to cover
75–90ml/5–6 tbsp olive oil
675g/1½lb boneless leg of pork, cut
   into large cubes
1 large onion, sliced
2 garlic cloves, chopped
400g/14oz can chopped tomatoes
grated rind of 1 orange
1 small dried red chilli
salt and ground black pepper

GL per serving: 13.5

1 Drain the chickpeas, rinse them under cold water and drain again. Place them in a large, heavy pan.

2 Pour in enough cold water to cover generously, put a lid on the pan and bring to the boil.

3 Skim the surface, replace the lid and cook gently for 1–1½ hours, depending on the age and quality of the chickpeas. Alternatively, cook them in a pressure cooker for 20 minutes under full pressure. When the chickpeas are soft, drain them, reserving the cooking liquid, and set them aside.

4 Heat the olive oil in the clean pan and brown the meat cubes in batches. As each cube browns, lift it out with a slotted spoon and put it on a plate.

5 When all the meat cubes have been browned, add the onion to the oil remaining in the pan and sauté the slices until softened and light golden in colour.

6 Stir in the garlic, then as soon as it becomes aromatic, add the tomatoes and orange rind.

7 Crumble in the chilli. Return the chickpeas and meat to the pan, and pour in enough of the reserved cooking liquid to cover. Season with black pepper, but not salt at this stage.

8 Mix well, cover and simmer for 1 hour, until the meat is tender. Stir occasionally and add more of the reserved liquid if needed. The result should be a moist casserole; not soupy, but not dry either. Season to taste with salt before serving.

Variation
To reduce the cooking time, use 2 x 400g/14oz cans of chickpeas, rinsed and drained, and omit steps 1–3. You will also need 450ml/ ¾ pint/2 cups light stock.

Energy 654kcal/2743kJ; Protein 56.4g; Carbohydrate 52.4g, of which sugars 9.6g; Fat 25.7g, of which saturates 4.9g; Cholesterol 106mg; Calcium 178mg; Fibre 11.4g; Sodium 164mg; GI 28.9

Italian sausages with cannellini beans

Variations on the theme of sausage and bean stew are found in most countries around the world as an inexpensive, easy and hearty peasant dish. This low-GL dish is a meal in itself, but you could serve it with fresh, steamed seasonal green vegetables, such as broccoli, cabbage or spinach, to further add to your recommended daily vegetable intake.

Serves 4

15ml/1 tbsp sunflower oil
12 Italian spicy fresh pork sausages
50g/2oz pancetta or streaky (fatty)
    bacon, chopped
2 onions, quartered
2 garlic cloves, crushed
1 large red (bell) pepper, halved, seeded
    and sliced
2 x 400g/14oz cans chopped tomatoes
400g/14oz can cannellini beans, drained
    and rinsed
salt and ground black pepper

GL per serving: 5.0

1 Pour the oil into a flameproof casserole and add the sausages and pancetta or bacon. Cook over a medium heat for about 10 minutes, turning occasionally, until the pancetta or bacon is crispy and the sausages are golden brown. Be careful to moderate the heat – if it is too fierce the sausages will burst.

2 When cooked, use a slotted spoon to remove the sausages and pancetta from the casserole. Set aside.

3 Discard any excess fat and add the onions and crushed garlic. Cook for about 5 minutes over a high heat, stirring frequently. Add the sliced pepper and cook for 2–3 minutes.

4 Return the sausages and pancetta to the casserole and stir in the chopped tomatoes and cannellini beans.

5 Bring to the boil, then reduce the heat and cover the casserole. Simmer for about 20 minutes, stirring occasionally. Season to taste and serve immediately.

Energy 794kcal/3303kJ; Protein 27.8g; Carbohydrate 49g, of which sugars 20.2g; Fat 55.4g, of which saturates 20g; Cholesterol 79mg; Calcium 176mg; Fibre 11.1g; Sodium 1710mg; GI 13.3

Spicy beef koftas with chickpea purée

Wherever you go in the Middle East you will encounter these tasty, very low-GL kebabs served with chickpea purée. The task of pounding the meat – traditionally performed using a mortar and pestle – is much easier in a food processor. It takes just minutes to mould the mixture around the skewers, and they don't take long to cook. Serve with a mixed salad and pitta bread.

Serves 6

500g/1¼lb finely minced (ground) beef
1 onion, grated
10ml/2 tsp ground cumin
10ml/2 tsp ground coriander
10ml/2 tsp paprika
2.5ml/½ tsp cayenne pepper
5ml/1 tsp salt
small bunch of fresh flat leaf parsley,
   finely chopped
small bunch of fresh coriander (cilantro),
   finely chopped

For the chickpea purée
400g/14oz can chickpeas, drained
   and rinsed
50ml/2fl oz/¼ cup olive oil
juice of 1 lemon
2 garlic cloves, crushed
5ml/1 tsp cumin seeds
30ml/2 tbsp light tahini paste
60ml/4 tbsp thick Greek (US strained
   plain) yogurt
a little olive oil, for drizzling
salt and ground black pepper

GL per serving: 0.4

1 Mix the minced beef with the onion, ground cumin, coriander, paprika, cayenne, salt, chopped parsley and chopped fresh coriander.

2 Knead the mixture, then pound it until smooth in a mortar with a pestle or in a blender or food processor. Place in a dish, cover and leave to stand in a cool place for 1 hour.

3 Preheat the oven to 200°C/400°F/ Gas 6. Meanwhile, make the chickpea purée. In a blender or food processor, process the chickpeas with the olive oil, lemon juice, garlic, cumin seeds, tahini and yogurt until well mixed.

4 Season with salt and pepper, tip the purée into an ovenproof dish, cover with foil and heat through in the oven for 15–20 minutes.

5 Preheat the grill (broiler) on the hottest setting. Divide the meat mixture into six portions and mould each equal portion on to a metal skewer, so that the meat resembles a fat sausage. Cook the kebabs for 4–5 minutes on each side, or until cooked through.

6 Drizzle a little olive oil over the hot chickpea purée, then serve immediately with the kebabs.

Variation
For a cheat's chickpea purée, use a supermarket hummus, and mix in a little lemon juice and Greek (US strained plain) yogurt.

Energy 376kcal/1562kJ; Protein 23g; Carbohydrate 12.6g, of which sugars 1.8g; Fat 26.3g, of which saturates 7.6g; Cholesterol 50mg; Calcium 108mg; Fibre 3.7g; Sodium 226mg; GI 2.3

North African beef stew with peas

This is a fabulous dish to make for family meals or easy entertaining, especially when fresh peas are in season. Like dried peas, fresh green peas are a good source of low-GL carbohydrate and provide valuable dietary fibre. Frozen peas could be used instead. Saffron, ginger and preserved lemon all contribute to the exciting flavour, and olives enhance the appeal.

Serves 6

1.2kg/2½lb chuck steak or stewing beef, trimmed and cubed
30ml/2 tbsp olive oil
1 onion, chopped
25g/1oz fresh root ginger, peeled and finely chopped
5ml/1 tsp ground ginger
pinch of cayenne pepper
pinch of saffron threads
1.2kg/2½lb shelled fresh peas
2 tomatoes, skinned and chopped
1 preserved lemon, chopped
a handful of brown Kalamata olives
salt and ground black pepper

GL per serving: 16.3

1 Put the cubed meat in a tagine, flameproof casserole or heavy pan with the olive oil, onion, fresh and ground ginger, cayenne and saffron, and season with salt and pepper. Pour in enough water to cover the meat and then bring to the boil.

2 Reduce the heat and then cover and simmer for about 1½ hours, until the meat is very tender. Cook for a little longer, if necessary.

3 Add the peas, tomatoes, preserved lemon and olives. Stir well and cook, uncovered, for about 10 minutes, or until the peas are just tender, the tomatoes have cooked down and the sauce has reduced.

4 Taste to check the seasoning, then serve immediately.

Energy 575kcal/2393kJ; Protein 59.7g; Carbohydrate 24.4g, of which sugars 6.2g; Fat 27.2g, of which saturates 9g; Cholesterol 116mg; Calcium 67mg; Fibre 10.4g; Sodium 508mg; GI 45.9

Lamb and carrot casserole with barley

Barley and carrots make natural partners for flavoursome lamb and mutton. In this convenient casserole the barley, a low-GL grain, makes the meat stretch further and adds to the flavour and texture as well as thickening the sauce. The dish is comfort food at its best. Serve with boiled new potatoes or a baked potato and a seasonal green vegetable, such as spring cabbage.

Serves 6

675g/1½lb lean stewing lamb
15ml/1 tbsp vegetable oil
2 onions, sliced
675g/1½lb carrots, thickly sliced
4–6 celery sticks, sliced
45ml/3 tbsp pearl or pot barley, rinsed
600ml/1 pint/2½ cups stock or water
salt and ground black pepper
chopped fresh parsley, to garnish

GL per serving: 2.9

1 Trim the lamb and cut it into bitesize pieces. Heat the oil in a flameproof casserole and brown the lamb.

2 Add the vegetables to the casserole and fry them briefly with the meat. Add the barley and enough stock or water to cover. Season with salt and pepper.

3 Cover the casserole and simmer gently or cook in a slow oven, 150°C/300°F/Gas 2 for 1–1½ hours until the meat is tender. Add extra stock or water during cooking if necessary.

4 Serve garnished with the chopped fresh parsley.

Energy 302kcal/1264kJ; Protein 23.9g; Carbohydrate 19.1g, of which sugars 11.1g; Fat 15g, of which saturates 6.2g; Cholesterol 86mg; Calcium 51mg; Fibre 3.4g; Sodium 127mg; GI 22.2

salads
and
side dishes

Most vegetables are low GL and should be eaten
freely as part of a healthy diet. This section
includes side salads and cooked vegetable dishes
to serve as accompaniments, including a split pea
and shallot mash that makes a low-GL alternative
to potatoes. The watermelon and feta cheese,
and white bean salads would also both make
great appetizers or light meals.

Beetroot and red onion salad

This salad looks especially attractive when made with a mixture of red and golden beetroot.
Try serving it with lean roast beef or cooked ham for an appealing and very low-GL light meal.

Serves 6

500g/1¼lb small beetroot (beets)
75ml/5 tbsp water
60ml/4 tbsp olive oil
90g/3½oz/scant 1 cup walnut or
   pecan halves
5ml/1 tsp caster (superfine) sugar,
   plus a little extra for the dressing
30ml/2 tbsp walnut oil
15ml/1 tbsp sherry vinegar or
   balsamic vinegar
5ml/1 tsp soy sauce
5ml/1 tsp grated orange rind
2.5ml/½ tsp ground roasted
   coriander seeds
5–10ml/1–2 tsp orange juice
1 red onion, halved and very
   thinly sliced
75g/3oz watercress or mizuna leaves
salt and ground black pepper

GL per serving: 0.9

1 Preheat the oven to 180°C/350°F/
Gas 4. Place the beetroot in an ovenproof dish large enough to hold them
in a single layer and add the water.

2 Cover the dish and cook in the oven
for about 1–1½ hours, or until the
beetroot are just tender.

3 Cool, then peel the beetroot, then
slice and cut them into strips and
toss with 15ml/1 tbsp of the olive oil.
Transfer to a bowl and set aside.

4 Meanwhile, heat 15ml/1 tbsp olive
oil in a frying pan and cook the walnuts
or pecans until they begin to brown.
Add the sugar and cook, stirring
continuously, until the nuts begin to
caramelize. Season with a pinch of salt
and lots of pepper, then turn the nuts
out on to a plate to cool completely.

5 Whisk together the remaining olive
oil, the walnut oil, vinegar, soy sauce,
orange rind and coriander to make the
dressing. Season and add a pinch of
sugar. Whisk in the orange juice.

6 Add the sliced red onion to the strips
of beetroot, then pour over the dressing
and toss thoroughly to mix.

7 When ready to serve, toss the salad
with the watercress or mizuna. Transfer
to individual bowls, sprinkle with the
caramelized nuts and serve.

Energy 239kcal/991kJ; Protein 3.3g; Carbohydrate 8.2g, of which sugars 7.2g; Fat 21.7g, of which saturates 2.3g; Cholesterol 0mg; Calcium 50mg; Fibre 2.6g; Sodium 121mg; GI 1.8

Watermelon and feta cheese salad

This refreshing salad is ideal for warm summer months. Watermelon has a low GL value (although it scores highly on the GI index), as a portion size is low in carbohydrate.

Serves 4

30–45ml/2–3 tbsp olive oil
juice of ½ lemon
5ml/1 tsp wine or cider vinegar
sprinkling of fresh thyme
pinch of ground cumin
4 large slices of watermelon, chilled
1 frisée lettuce, core removed
130g/4½oz feta cheese, preferably sheep's
    milk feta, cut into bitesize pieces
handful of lightly toasted pumpkin seeds
handful of sunflower seeds
12–16 black olives

GL per serving: 6.4

1 Pour the olive oil, lemon juice and vinegar into a bowl or jug (pitcher). Add the fresh thyme and ground cumin, and whisk until well combined. Set the dressing aside until you are ready to serve the salad.

2 Cut the rind off the watermelon and remove as many of the seeds as possible. Cut the flesh into triangular-shaped chunks.

3 Just before serving, put the lettuce leaves in a bowl, pour over the dressing and toss together.

4 Arrange the leaves on a serving dish or individual plates and add the watermelon and feta cheese.

5 Sprinkle the pumpkin and sunflower seeds and black olives over the top, and serve the salad immediately.

Energy 256kcal/1066kJ; Protein 7.7g; Carbohydrate 12.9g, of which sugars 11.6g; Fat 19.7g, of which saturates 6.2g; Cholesterol 23mg; Calcium 165mg; Fibre 1.4g; Sodium 616mg; GI 54.7

White beans with green pepper in a spicy dressing

Tender, low-GL white beans are delicious combined with this chilli and garlic dressing and the bite of fresh green pepper. Serve with strips of lightly toasted pitta bread as a light meal.

Serves 4

750g/1⅔lb tomatoes, diced
1 onion, finely chopped
½–1 mild fresh chilli, finely chopped
1 green (bell) pepper, seeded and chopped
pinch of sugar
4 garlic cloves, chopped
400g/14oz can butter (lima) or cannellini beans, drained
45–60ml/3–4 tbsp olive oil
grated rind and juice of 1 lemon
15ml/1 tbsp cider vinegar or wine vinegar
salt and ground black pepper
chopped fresh parsley, to garnish

GL per serving: 14.9

1 Put the diced tomatoes, chopped onion, chilli, green pepper, sugar, garlic, butter or cannellini beans, salt and plenty of freshly ground black pepper in a large bowl and toss together with wooden spoons until the mixture is well combined.

2 Whisk the oil, lemon rind, lemon juice and vinegar together in a jug (pitcher). Add to the salad and toss lightly to combine well.

3 Chill in the refrigerator before serving, garnished with chopped parsley.

Energy 226kcal/947kJ; Protein 8.8g; Carbohydrate 27.6g, of which sugars 12.9g; Fat 9.6g, of which saturates 1.5g; Cholesterol 0mg; Calcium 92mg; Fibre 9g; Sodium 409mg; GI 21.1

Lemony couscous, olive and courgette salad

This medium-GL salad combines olives, almonds and courgettes with couscous and a herb, lemon juice and olive oil dressing. It makes a sustaining accompaniment to grilled fish or meat.

Serves 4

275g/10oz/1⅔ cups couscous
550ml/18fl oz/2½ cups boiling
   vegetable stock
2 small courgettes (zucchini)
16–20 black olives
25g/1oz/¼ cup flaked (sliced) almonds, toasted
60ml/4 tbsp olive oil
15ml/1 tbsp lemon juice
15ml/1 tbsp chopped fresh coriander (cilantro)
15ml/1 tbsp chopped fresh parsley
a good pinch of ground cumin
a good pinch of cayenne pepper

GL per serving: 19.5

3 Fluff up the couscous with a fork, then stir in the strips of courgette, the olives and the toasted almonds, and toss everything together.

4 Whisk the olive oil, lemon juice, coriander, parsley, cumin and cayenne in a bowl. Stir into the salad and toss. Transfer to a serving dish and serve.

1 Place the couscous in a large bowl and pour over the boiling stock. Stir and then set aside for 10 minutes until all the stock has been absorbed.

2 Meanwhile, trim the courgettes and cut them into pieces about 2.5cm/1in long. Slice into fine julienne strips with a sharp knife. Halve the black olives, discarding the pits.

Energy 337kcal/1398kJ; Protein 7.3g; Carbohydrate 37.5g, of which sugars 2g; Fat 18.3g, of which saturates 2.4g; Cholesterol 0mg; Calcium 68mg; Fibre 2.1g; Sodium 565mg; GI 53.2

Spring vegetables with tarragon

A combination of vegetables always looks especially appealing and this medley makes the most of the seasonal spring choices. Fresh tarragon adds a wonderful depth to this bright, fresh, low-GL dish. It goes well as an accompaniment to fish and shellfish dishes.

Serves 4

1 bunch spring onions (scallions)
25g/1oz/2 tbsp butter
15ml/1 tbsp olive oil
1 garlic clove, crushed
115g/4oz asparagus tips
115g/4oz mangetouts (snowpeas), trimmed
115g/4oz young broad (fava) beans
2 Little Gem (Bibb) lettuces
15ml/1 tbsp finely chopped fresh tarragon
salt and ground black pepper

GL per serving: 1.7

1 Cut the spring onions into quarters. Gently heat the butter and oil in a large frying pan and fry the onions gently with the garlic.

2 Add the asparagus tips, mangetouts and broad beans. Mix in, covering all the pieces with oil.

3 Just cover the base of the pan with water, season, and allow to simmer gently for a few minutes.

4 Cut the lettuce into quarters and add to the pan. Cook for 3 minutes, or until all the vegetables are just tender. Sprinkle with the tarragon, then serve.

Energy 124kcal/515kJ; Protein 5.1g; Carbohydrate 6.8g, of which sugars 3.5g; Fat 8.7g, of which saturates 3.8g; Cholesterol 13mg; Calcium 62mg; Fibre 3.9g; Sodium 44mg; GI 50.4

Braised lettuce and peas

This is based on the traditional French way of cooking young greens so that their full flavour is appreciated. It's ideally made in spring and early summer, but could be made throughout the year using frozen peas. It makes a delicious low-GL accompaniment to grilled chicken.

Serves 4

25g/1oz/2 tbsp butter
4 Little Gem (Bibb) lettuces,
   halved lengthways
2 bunches spring onions (scallions), trimmed
   and cut into 5cm/2in lengths
5ml/1 tsp caster (superfine) sugar
400g/14oz shelled peas (about 1kg/2¼lb
   in pods)
4 fresh mint sprigs
120ml/4fl oz/½ cup chicken or vegetable
   stock or water
15ml/1 tbsp chopped fresh mint
salt and ground black pepper

GL per serving: 5.5

1 Gently melt the butter over a low heat in a large pan. Add the prepared lettuces and spring onions.

2 Turn the vegetables in the butter to coat completely, then add the sugar, 2.5ml/½ tsp salt and plenty of ground black pepper.

3 Cover and cook very gently for about 5 minutes, stirring once. Add the peas and mint sprigs. Turn the peas in the buttery juices and pour in the stock or water, then cover and cook over a gentle heat for a further 5 minutes.

4 Uncover and increase the heat to reduce the liquid to a few tablespoons.

5 Remove the mint sprigs, then toss the vegetables with the chopped fresh mint. Transfer to a warmed serving dish and serve immediately.

Variations
• Braise about 250g/9oz baby carrots with the lettuce.
• Fry 115g/4oz chopped pancetta or streaky (fatty) bacon with one small chopped onion in the butter.

Energy 161kcal/670kJ; Protein 9.1g; Carbohydrate 15.9g, of which sugars 6.8g; Fat 7.4g, of which saturates 3.7g; Cholesterol 13mg; Calcium 73mg; Fibre 6.5g; Sodium 47mg; GI 43.0

Tomato and potato bake

Although your intake of potatoes should be limited on a low-GL diet, they can be enjoyed occasionally. The best potatoes to use are those with a waxy texture, as they not only hold their shape well, but also have a lower GL than floury varieties. This is a convenient dish that can be left to cook and it makes a tasty accompaniment to grilled fish, chicken or lean meat.

Serves 6

120ml/4fl oz/½ cup olive oil
1 large onion, finely chopped
3 garlic cloves, crushed
4 large ripe tomatoes, peeled, seeded
  and chopped
1kg/2¼lb even-size main-crop waxy potatoes
salt and ground black pepper
fresh flat leaf parsley, chopped, to garnish

GL per serving: 12.6

Cook's tip
To peel tomatoes, place in a heatproof bowl and cover with boiling water. Leave for 1 minute, then peel off the skins using a knife.

1 Heat the oil in a flameproof casserole. Fry the chopped onion and garlic for 5 minutes, or until softened and just starting to brown.

2 Add the tomatoes to the casserole, season and cook for 1 minute.

3 Preheat the oven to 180°C/350°F/ Gas 4.

4 Cut the potatoes into wedges. Add to the casserole, stirring well. Cook for 10 minutes. Season again with salt and pepper, and cover with a tight-fitting lid.

5 Place the covered casserole in the oven and cook for 45 minutes to 1 hour, until the potatoes are tender. Garnish with chopped fresh flat leaf parsley and serve immediately.

Energy 264kcal/1107kJ; Protein 4.1g; Carbohydrate 34.2g, of which sugars 8g; Fat 13.3g, of which saturates 2g; Cholesterol 0mg; Calcium 31mg; Fibre 3.3g; Sodium 26mg; GI 43.6

Split pea and shallot mash

Greatly underrated and underused, split peas can make a fantastic purée. When this is enlivened with herbs and spices, the purée makes an excellent low-GL alternative to mashed potatoes, and is a particularly good accompaniment to casseroles and nut roasts. It can also be served with warm pitta bread and plenty of diced ripe tomatoes.

Serves 4–6

225g/8oz/1 cup yellow split peas
1 bay leaf
8 sage leaves, roughly chopped
30ml/2 tbsp olive oil
3 shallots, finely chopped
10ml/2 tsp cumin seeds
1 large garlic clove, chopped
salt and ground black pepper

GL per serving: 9.2

1 Place the split peas in a bowl and cover with cold water. Leave to soak for 1–2 hours, then drain in a sieve (strainer), rinse, and drain again.

2 Place the peas in a large pan, cover with fresh cold water and bring to the boil. Skim off any foam that rises to the surface, then reduce the heat.

3 Add the bay leaf and sage, and simmer for 30–40 minutes until the peas are tender. Add more water during cooking, if necessary.

4 Meanwhile, heat the oil in a frying pan and cook the shallots, cumin seeds and garlic for 3 minutes or until the shallots soften, stirring occasionally. Add the mixture to the split peas while they are still cooking.

5 Drain the split peas, reserving the cooking water.

6 Remove the bay leaf, then place the split pea mixture in a food processor or blender.

7 Add 105ml/7 tbsp of the reserved cooking water and blend until the mixture forms a coarse purée. Add more water if it seems to be too dry. Season to taste and serve warm.

Cook's tip

It is not essential to soak split peas; it really depends on how long they have been stored for. Soaking will, however, speed up the cooking time. Green split peas or split lentils could also be used in this recipe.

Energy 156kcal/658kJ; Protein 9.1g; Carbohydrate 21.9g, of which sugars 1.5g; Fat 4.2g, of which saturates 0.6g; Cholesterol 0mg; Calcium 22mg; Fibre 2g; Sodium 14mg; GI 27.3

desserts and sweet snacks

For most days, fresh fruit or yogurt makes a good low-GL choice as a dessert or sweet snack. However, for special occasions, sweet treats needn't be totally omitted. The recipes in this section are all fruit-based and so require only a little added honey or sugar to taste. So enjoy a delicious oat-topped fruit crumble, baked or poached fruits or a soufflé omelette with strawberries.

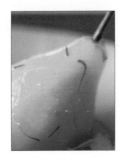

Grapefruit salad with minted pomegranate yogurt

The jewel-like, ruby red seeds of the pomegranate make any dessert look beautiful. Here they are stirred into yogurt to make a delicate sauce for a fresh-tasting low-GL grapefruit salad.

Serves 3–4

300ml/½ pint/1¼ cups Greek
(US strained plain) yogurt
2–3 ripe pomegranates
30ml/2 tbsp fresh mint, chopped
10ml/2 tsp clear honey
fresh mint leaves, to decorate

For the grapefruit salad
2 red grapefruits
2 pink grapefruits
1 white grapefruit
15–30ml/1–2 tbsp orange
flower water
caster (superfine) sugar,
to taste (optional)

GL per serving: 4.3

1 Beat the yogurt in a bowl. Cut open the pomegranates and scoop out the seeds, removing and discarding all the pith. Fold the pomegranate seeds into the yogurt, reserving a few of the seeds for decoration. Stir in the mint, then the honey. Chill.

2 Peel the red, pink and white grapefruits, cutting off and discarding all the pith. Cut between the membranes to remove the segments, holding the fruit over a bowl to catch the juices.

3 Discard the membranes and mix the fruit segments with the reserved juices. Sprinkle with the orange flower water and add a little caster sugar to sweeten, if liked. Stir gently to combine, then cover and chill.

4 Decorate the chilled yogurt with a sprinkling of the reserved pomegranate seeds and mint leaves, and serve with the grapefruit salad.

Energy 193kcal/809kJ; Protein 6.1g; Carbohydrate 25.8g, of which sugars 25.6g; Fat 7.9g, of which saturates 5.1g; Cholesterol 13mg; Calcium 144mg; Fibre 3.8g; Sodium 57mg; GI 29.2

Crunchy rolled oat, yogurt and raspberry cranachan

This tempting low-GL dessert is based on a traditional Scottish recipe, but uses Greek yogurt instead of cream. A mixture of seasonal berries could be used, depending on what is available.

Serves 4

75g/3oz crunchy oat cereal
600ml/1 pint/2½ cups Greek
   (US strained plain) yogurt
250g/9oz/1½ cups raspberries

GL per serving: 2.3

1 Preheat the grill (broiler) to high. Spread the oat cereal on a baking sheet and place under the hot grill for 3–4 minutes until lightly toasted, stirring regularly. Set aside to cool.

2 When the oat cereal has cooled completely, fold it into the Greek yogurt.

3 Gently fold 200g/7oz/generous 1 cup of the raspberries into the yogurt mixture, being careful not to crush the berries too much.

4 Spoon the yogurt mixture into four serving glasses or dishes, top with the remaining raspberries and serve the cranachan immediately.

Energy 242kcal/1013kJ; Protein 10g; Carbohydrate 21.7g, of which sugars 15.6g; Fat 13.4g, of which saturates 7.2g; Cholesterol 21mg; Calcium 255mg; Fibre 2.5g; Sodium 241mg; GI 13.0

Soufflé omelette with strawberries

A light and fluffy soufflé omelette filled with fresh, juicy strawberries makes a luscious treat for every occasion. It is also really quick and easy to make and has a very low GL.

Serves 3

75g/3oz/¾ cup strawberries
3 eggs, separated
30ml/2 tbsp caster (superfine) sugar
45ml/3 tbsp double (heavy) cream,
   lightly whipped
a few drops of vanilla extract
25g/1oz/2 tbsp butter

GL per serving: 0.5

Variations
Use any type of soft fruit in place of the strawberries. Slices of peach, berries or a combination of several fruits will all work well.

1 Wash and hull the strawberries, then cut them in half and set aside. In a bowl, beat the egg yolks and sugar until pale and fluffy, then fold in the cream and vanilla extract.

2 Whisk the egg whites in a very large, grease-free bowl until stiff, then carefully fold into the yolk mixture.

3 Melt the butter in a large omelette pan. When sizzling, pour in the egg mixture and cook until set, shaking occasionally. Sprinkle the strawberries over one half.

4 Slide on to a warm serving plate, folding it over as it leaves the pan. Cut into three and serve immediately.

Energy 256kcal/1063kJ; Protein 6.8g; Carbohydrate 12.3g, of which sugars 12.3g; Fat 20.5g, of which saturates 10.9g; Cholesterol 229mg; Calcium 47mg; Fibre 0.3g; Sodium 126mg; GI 5.0

Nectarines baked with nuts

In this low-GL dessert, nectarines are stuffed with a ground almond and chopped pistachio nut filling and baked in orange juice, then served with an orange and passion fruit sauce.

Serves 4

50g/2oz/½ cup ground almonds
15ml/1 tbsp caster (superfine) sugar
1 egg yolk
50g/2oz/½ cup shelled pistachio
    nuts, chopped
4 nectarines
200ml/7fl oz/scant 1 cup orange juice
2 ripe passion fruit
45ml/3 tbsp orange liqueur (optional)

GL per serving: 6.0

1 In a large bowl, mix together the ground almonds, sugar and egg yolk to make a paste, then stir in the chopped pistachio nuts.

2 Cut the nectarines in half and carefully remove the stones (pits).

3 Place the nectarine halves in a single layer in the base of a shallow ovenproof dish, then pile the ground almond and pistachio mixture into them, packing in plenty of filling.

4 Pour the orange juice around the nectarines, then cover the dish with foil and place in an unheated oven. Set the oven to 200°C/400°F/Gas 6 and cook for 15 minutes.

5 Remove the foil from the dish and bake for a further 5–10 minutes, or until the nectarines are soft. Transfer the nectarines to individual, warmed serving plates and keep warm.

6 Cut the passion fruit in half, scoop out the seeds and stir into the cooking juices in the dish with the orange liqueur, if using. Spoon the sauce over and around the nectarines and serve immediately.

Energy 277kcal/1159kJ; Protein 7.8g; Carbohydrate 21.9g, of which sugars 21.3g; Fat 15.5g, of which saturates 1.9g; Cholesterol 50mg; Calcium 66mg; Fibre 3.5g; Sodium 78mg; GI 30.2

Poached pears in scented honey syrup

In this healthy low-GL dish the poaching syrup is flavoured with saffron, cinnamon and lavender, producing an intriguing, exotic taste and aroma. Delicate and pretty to look at, these colourful scented pears would provide an exquisite finishing touch to any spicy meal, especially during the autumn or winter when pears are at their seasonal best.

Serves 4

45ml/3 tbsp clear honey
juice of 1 lemon
250ml/8fl oz/1 cup water
pinch of saffron threads
1 cinnamon stick
2–3 dried lavender heads
4 firm pears

GL per serving: 9.6

Variation
In summer, use whole nectarines or peaches instead of pears.

1 Heat the honey and lemon juice in a heavy pan that will hold the pears snugly. Stir over a gentle heat until the honey has dissolved.

2 Add the water, saffron threads, cinnamon stick and flowers from one or two lavender heads. Bring the mixture to the boil, then reduce the heat and simmer for 5 minutes.

3 Peel the pears, leaving the stalks attached. Add to the pan and simmer for 20 minutes, basting at regular intervals. Leave the pears to cool in the syrup and serve at room temperature, decorated with a few lavender flowers.

Energy 93kcal/392kJ; Protein 0.5g; Carbohydrate 23.6g, of which sugars 23.6g; Fat 0.2g, of which saturates 0g; Cholesterol 0mg; Calcium 17mg; Fibre 3.3g; Sodium 6mg; GI 43.9

Oat-topped rhubarb frushie

'Frushie' is the old Scots word for a crumble, and it makes a warming dessert during cold weather. In this instance the topping is made with rolled oats as well as flour, making a lower-GL mixture than if just flour was used. Other seasonal fruits, such as apple, apple and blackberry combined, gooseberries or plums, can be used according to preference and availability.

Serves 4

450g/1lb rhubarb or other fruit
50g/2oz/¼ cup caster (superfine) sugar
   or 30ml/2 tbsp redcurrant jelly
45–60ml/3–4 tbsp water
squeeze of lemon juice

For the crumble
50g/2oz/½ cup plain
   (all-purpose) flour
25g/1oz/scant ⅓ cup coarse
   rolled oats
50g/2oz/¼ cup soft light
   brown sugar
50g/2oz/¼ cup butter, softened

GL per serving: 9.25

1 Preheat the oven to 200°C/400°F/ Gas 6. Cook the rhubarb or other fruit with the sugar or redcurrant jelly, water and lemon juice for 15 minutes or until soft. Transfer to a deep pie dish.

2 Combine all the crumble ingredients with your fingers until the mixture has a crumb-like texture.

3 Sprinkle the crumble topping evenly over the fruit.

4 Bake at the top of the preheated oven for 20 minutes, or until the top is crunchy and slightly brown. Serve immediately with hot custard, Greek (US strained plain) yogurt or vanilla ice cream, if you like.

Energy 266kcal/1119kJ; Protein 3.1g; Carbohydrate 41g, of which sugars 27.4g; Fat 11.1g, of which saturates 6.6g; Cholesterol 27mg; Calcium 141mg; Fibre 2.4g; Sodium 82mg; GI 22.3

Index

Acknowledgements

Recipe writers:
Pepita Aris; Catherine Atkinson; Mridula Baljekar; Jane Bamforth; Alex Barker; Ghillie Basan; Judy Bastyra; Georgina Campbell; Trish Davies; Roz Denny; Coralie Dorman; Matthew Drennan; Joanna Farrow; Maria Filippelli; Jenni Fleetwood; Christine France; Yasuko Fukuoka; Elaine Gardner; Brian Glover; Nicola Graimes; Rosamund Grant; Carole Handslip; Juliet Harbutt; Rebekah Hassan; Simona Hill; Christine Ingram; Becky Johnson; Bridget Jones; Soheila Kimberley; Lucy Knox; Maggie Mayhew; Jane Milton; Suzannah Olivier; Keith Richmond; Rena Salaman; Marlena Spieler; Jane Stevenson; Liz Trigg; Linda Tubby; Sunil Vijayakar; Biddy White Lennon; Kate Whiteman; Jeni Wright.

Food stylists and home economists:
Alex Barker; Jacqueline Clarke; Annabel Ford; Wendy Lee; Lucy McKelvie; Emma MacIntosh; Emma Patmore; Bridget Sargeson; Jennie Shapter; Carol Tenant; Helen Trent; Linda Tubby; Sunil Vijayakar

Photographers:
Frank Adam; Karl Adamson; Edward Allwright; Peter Anderson; Tim Auty; Caroline Barty; Steve Baxter; Martin Brigdale; Louisa Dare; Nicky Dowey; James Duncan; Gus Filgate; Michelle Garrett; John Heseltine; Amanda Heywood; Janine Hosegood; Dave Jordan; Dave King; Don Last; William Lingwood; Patrick McLeavey; Michael Michaels; Thomas Odulate; Craig Robertson; Bridget Sargeson; Simon Smith; Sam Stowell.